JIRI GEORG DOKOUPIL

Làmpara, *39⅜ × 25½″, 100 × 65 cm., 1989*

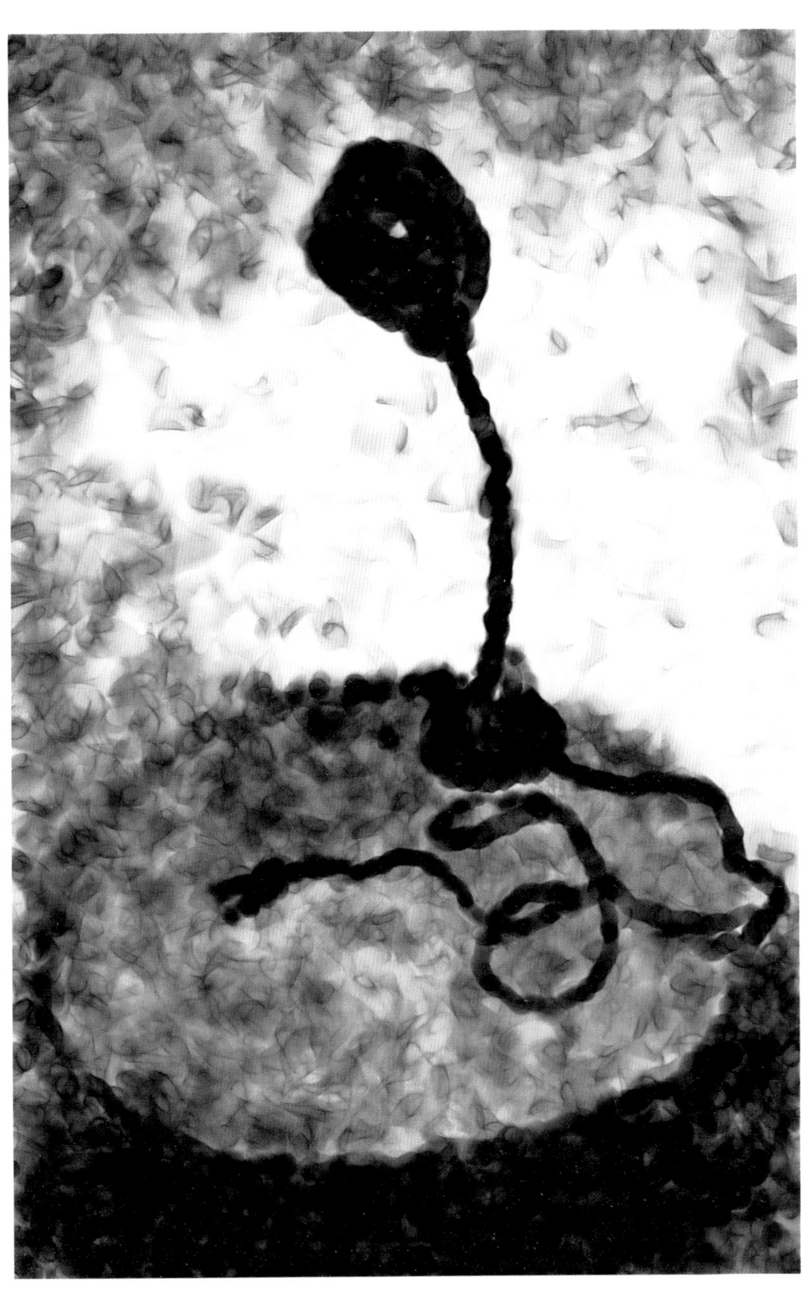

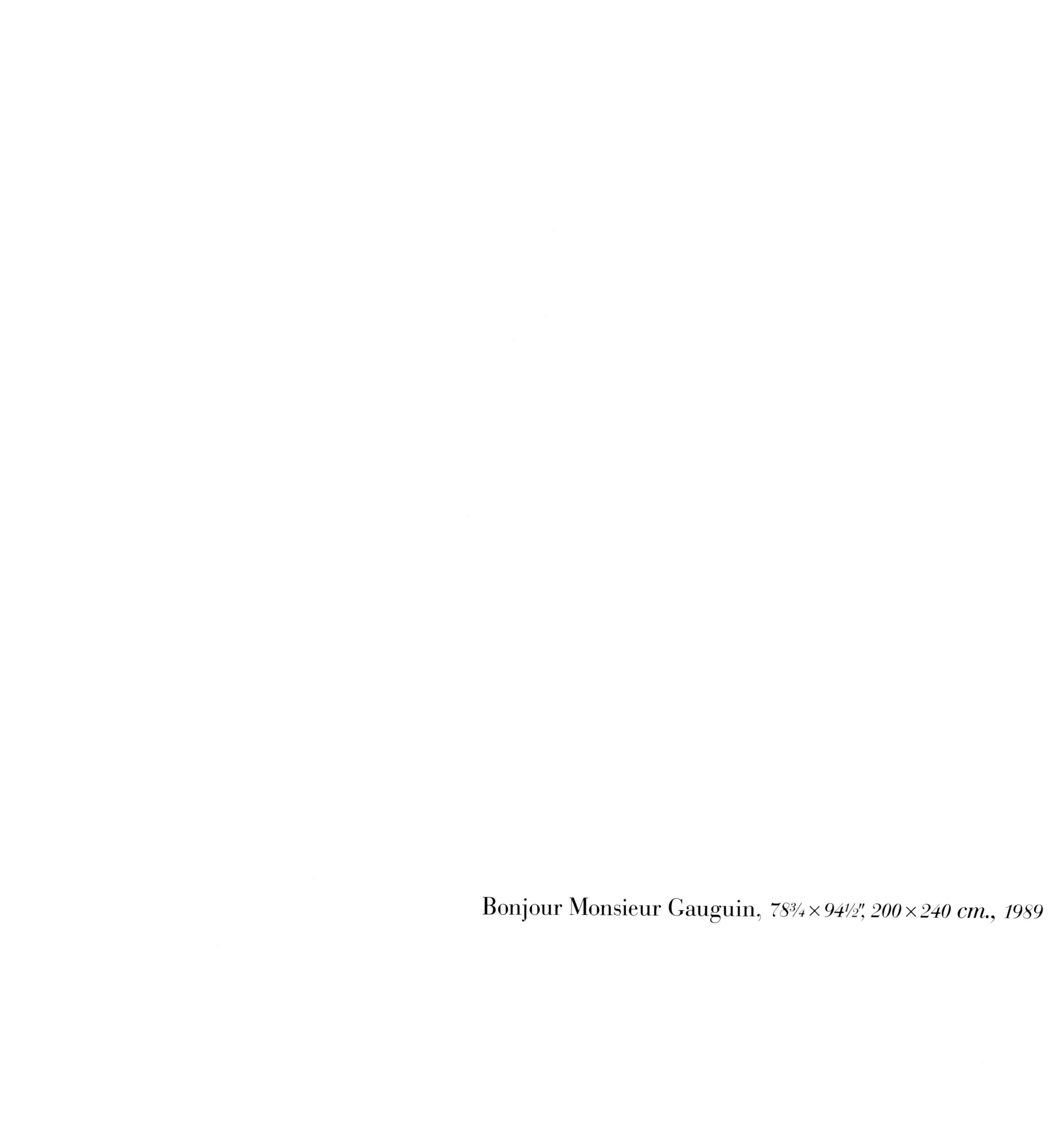

Bonjour Monsieur Gauguin, 78¾ × 94½", 200 × 240 cm., 1989

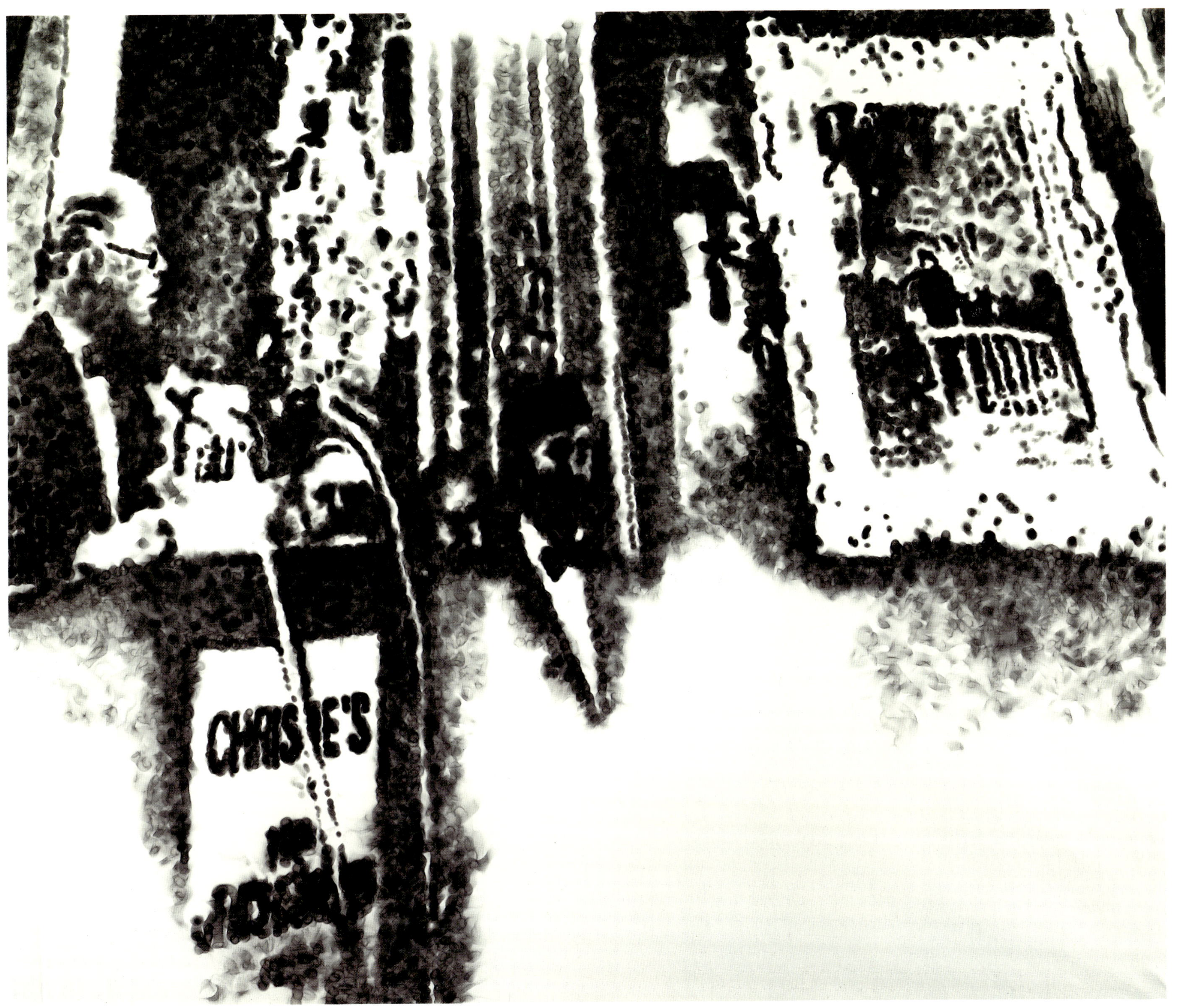

CHRISTIE'S

Gladiolos, *39⅜ × 31¾", 100 × 81 cm., 1989*

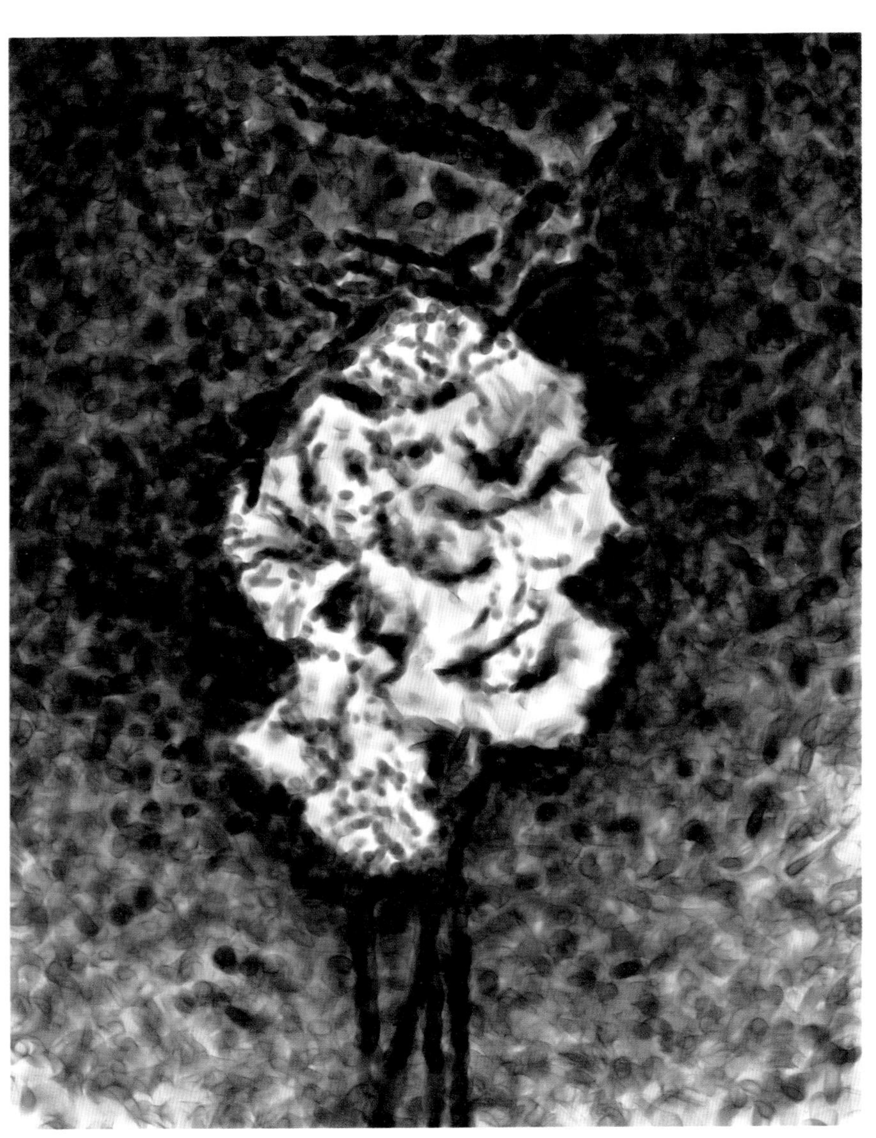

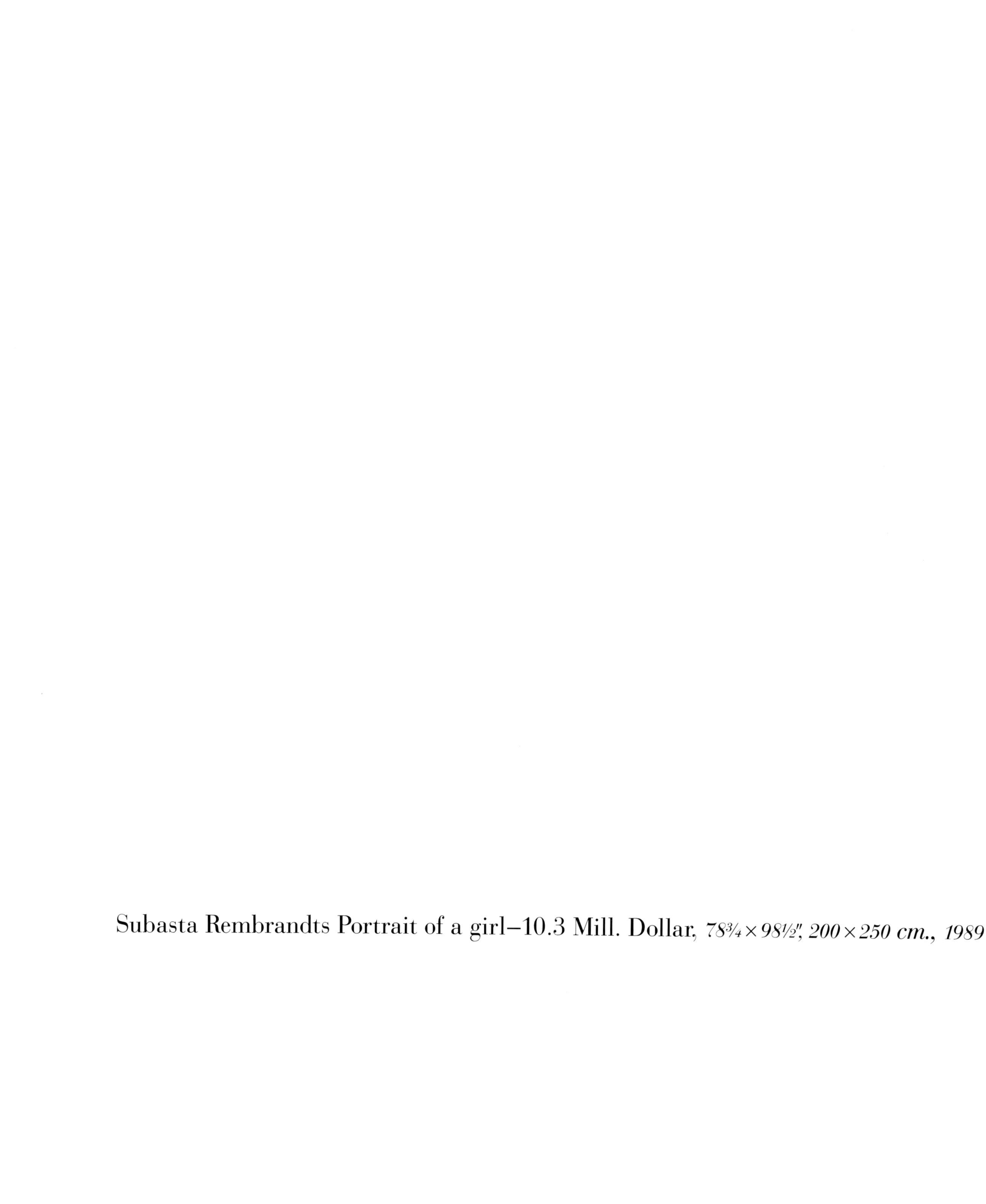

Subasta Rembrandts Portrait of a girl–10.3 Mill. Dollar, *78¾×98½", 200×250 cm., 1989*

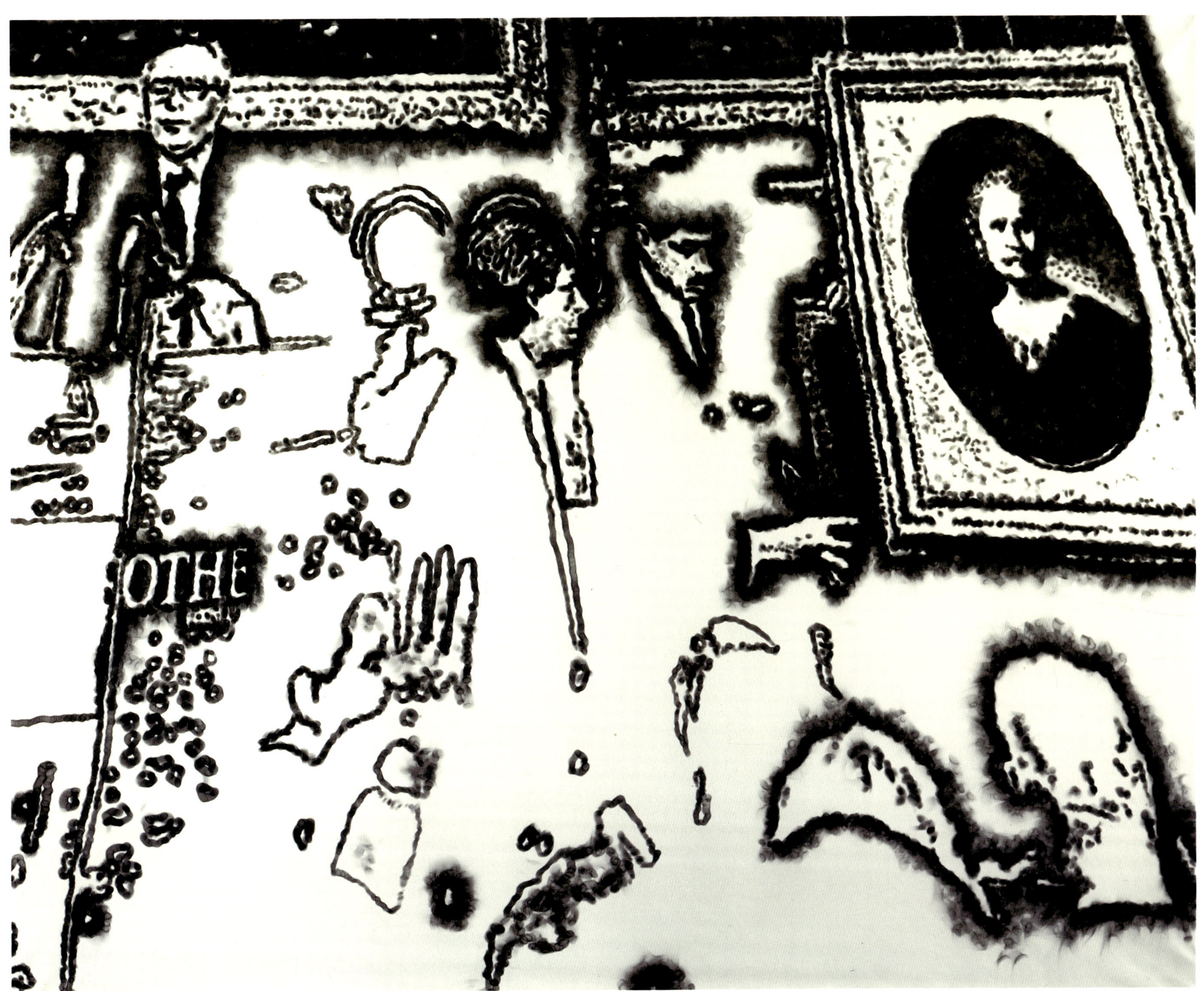

OTHE

El rincon, *39⅜ × 31¾″, 100 × 81 cm., 1989*

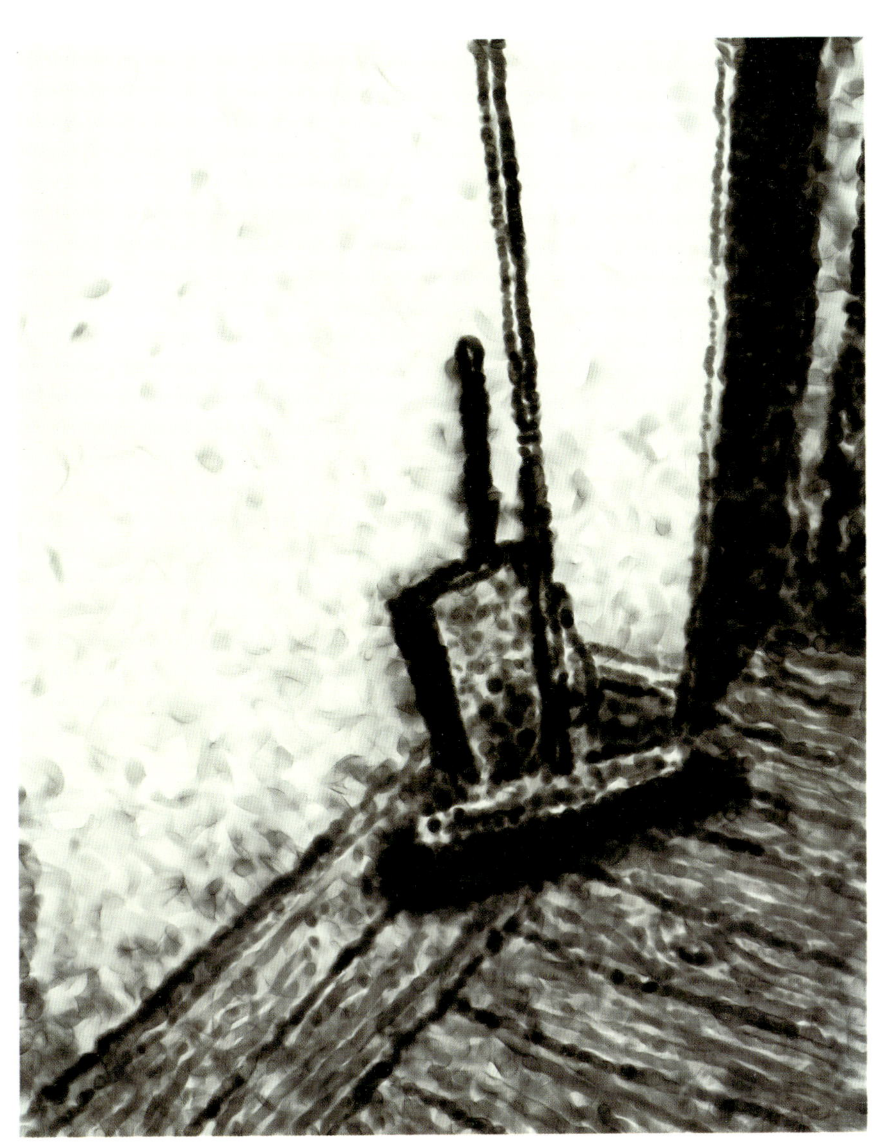

Auction at Christie's—Degas, 78¾ × 78¾", 200 × 200 cm., 1989

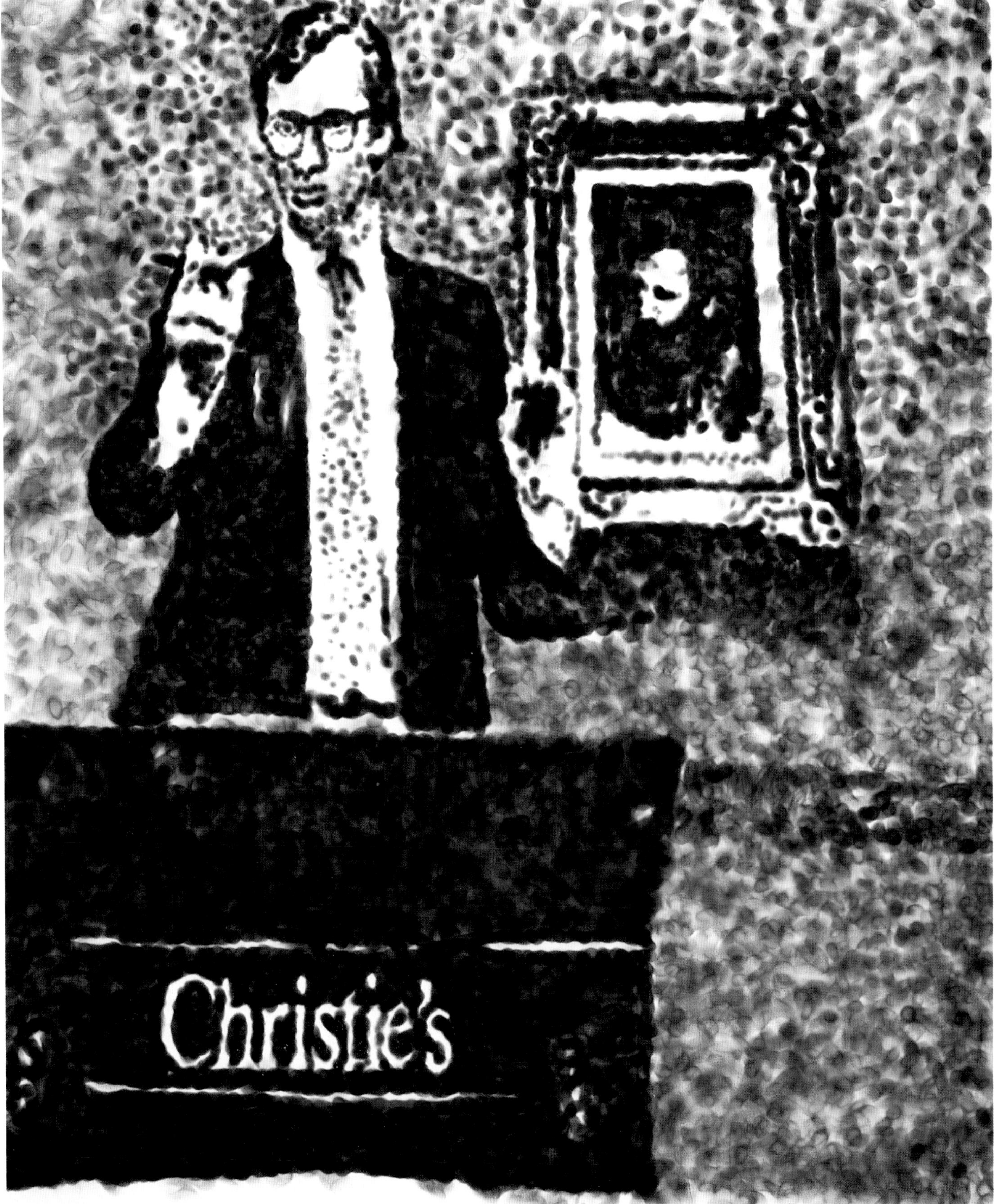

Christie's

Flores sobre una silla redonda, $39\frac{3}{8} \times 31\frac{3}{4}''$, 100×81 cm., 1989

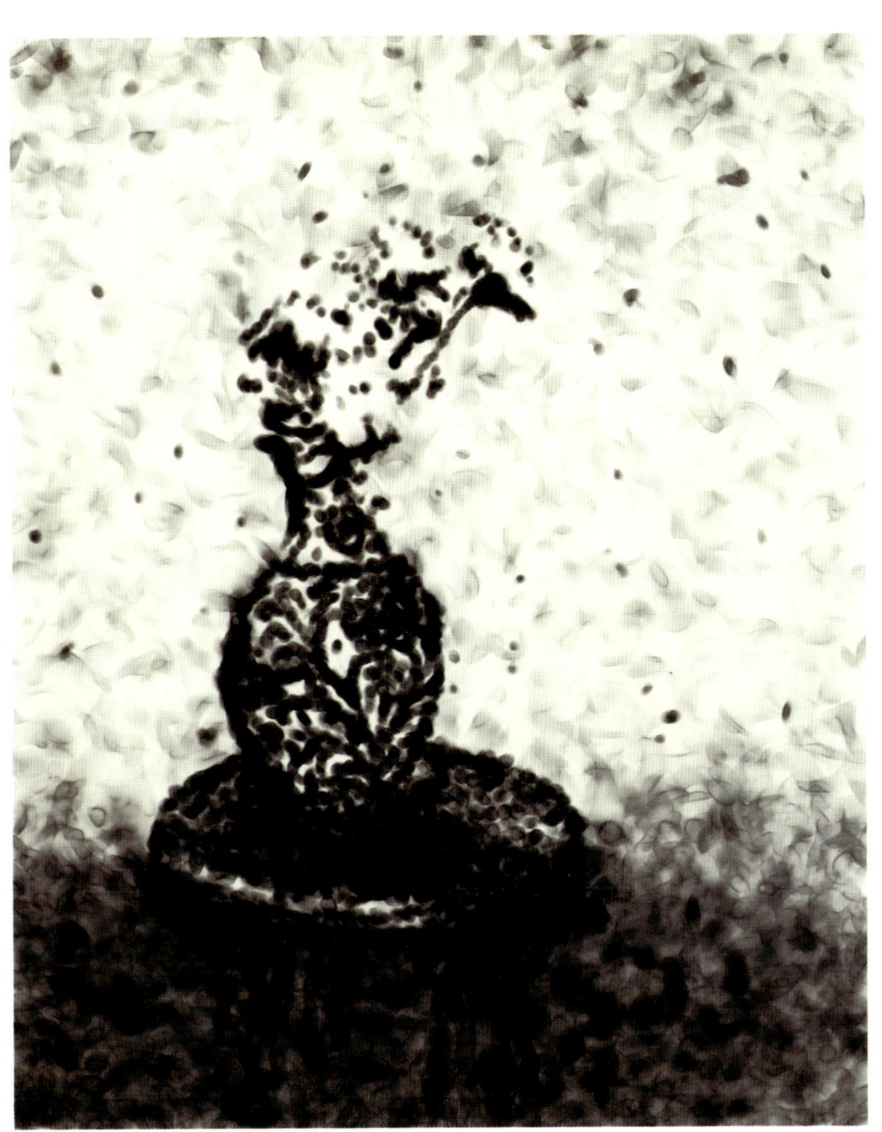

Subasta Toulouse Lautrec, 78¾ × 94½", 200 × 240 cm., 1989

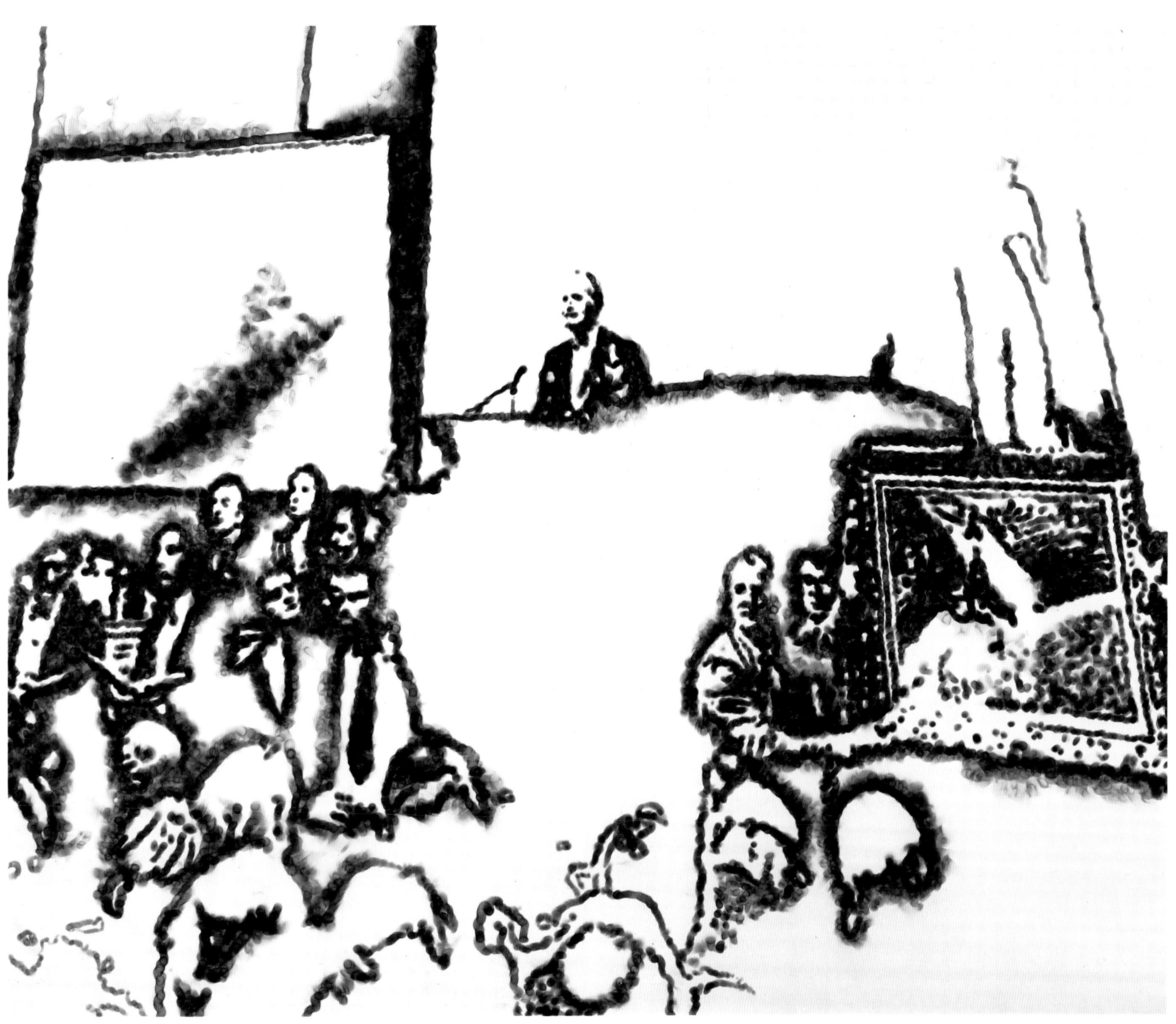

Torso, *39⅜ × 31¾", 100 × 81 cm., 1989*

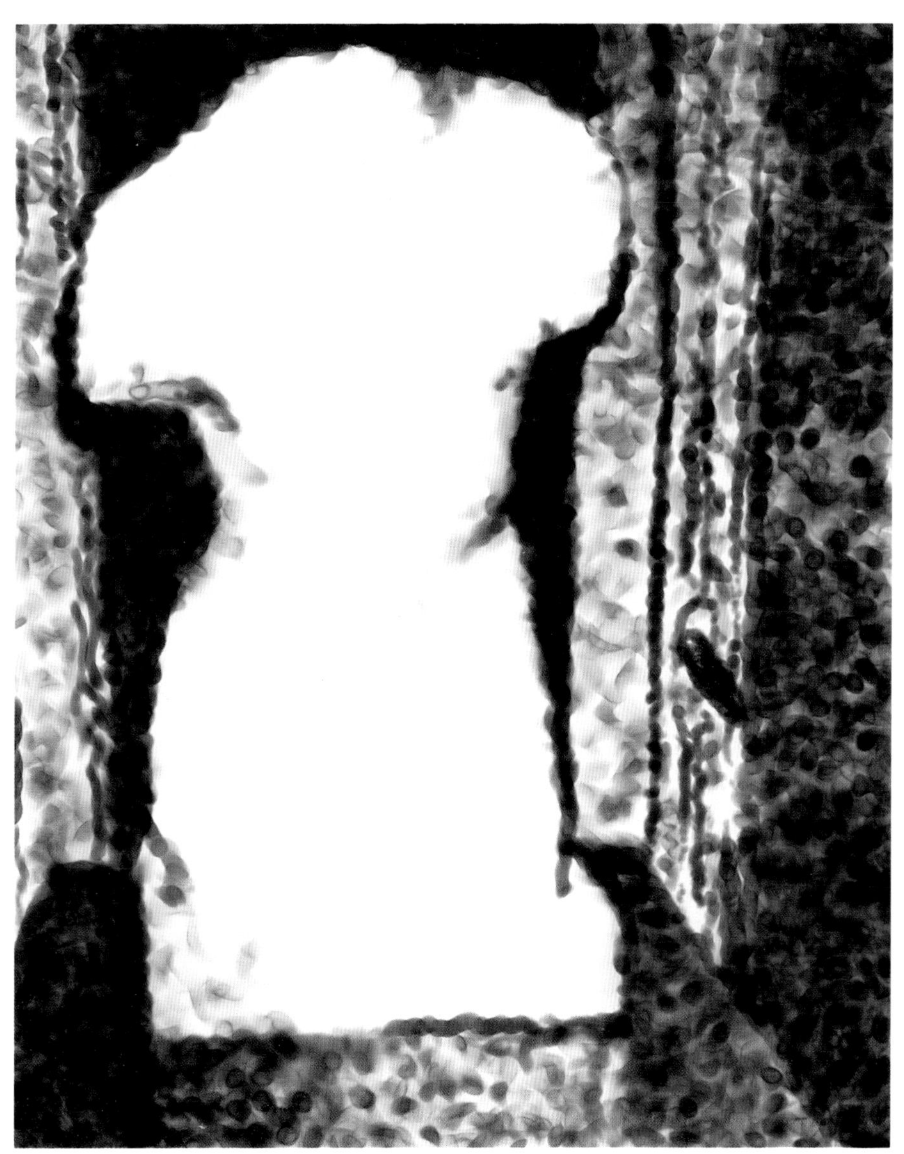

Subasta de Manet−11 Million Dollar, *98½ × 78¾", 250 × 200 cm., 1989*

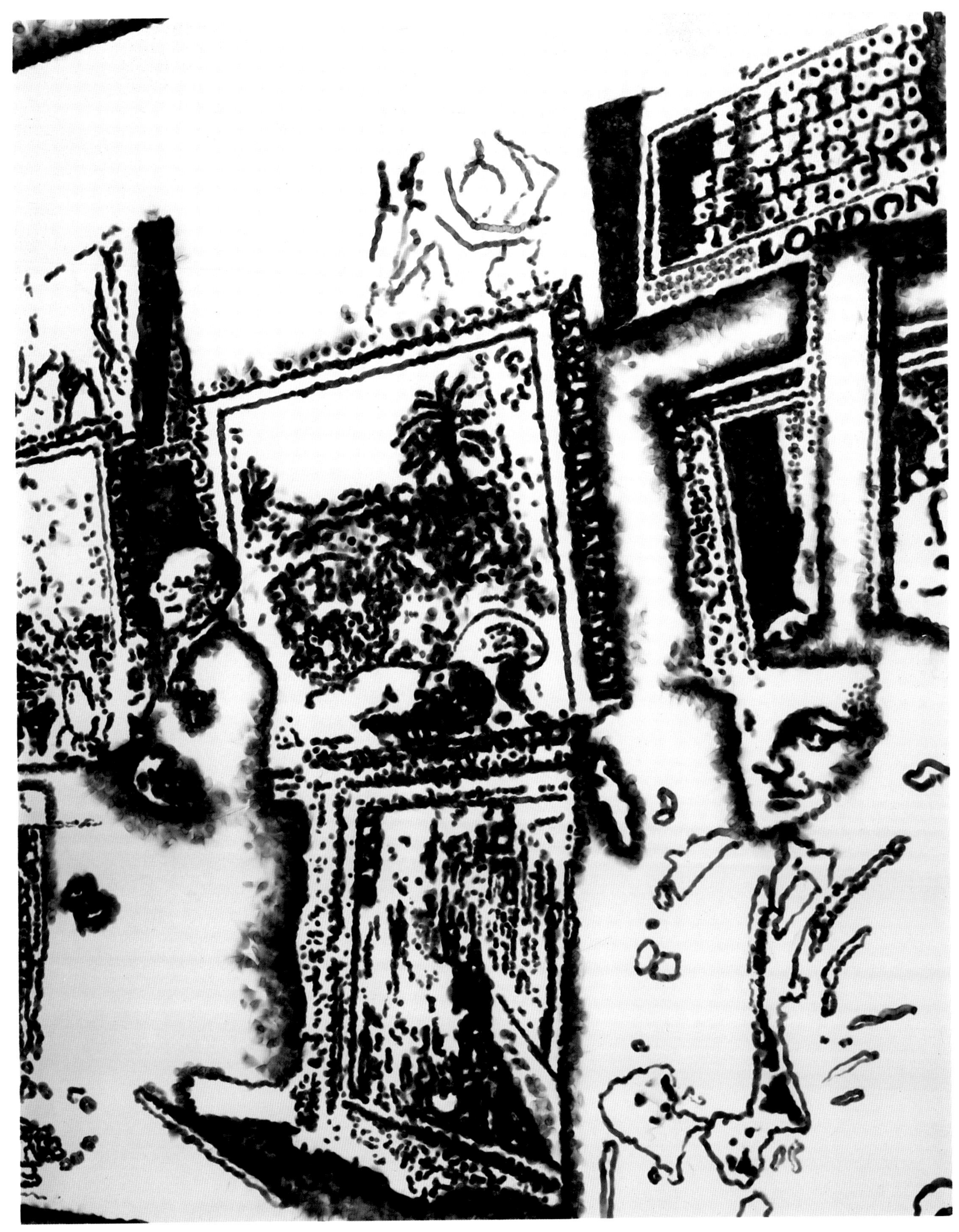

LONDON

Flores en un jarron, 39⅜ × 31¾", 100 × 81 cm., 1989

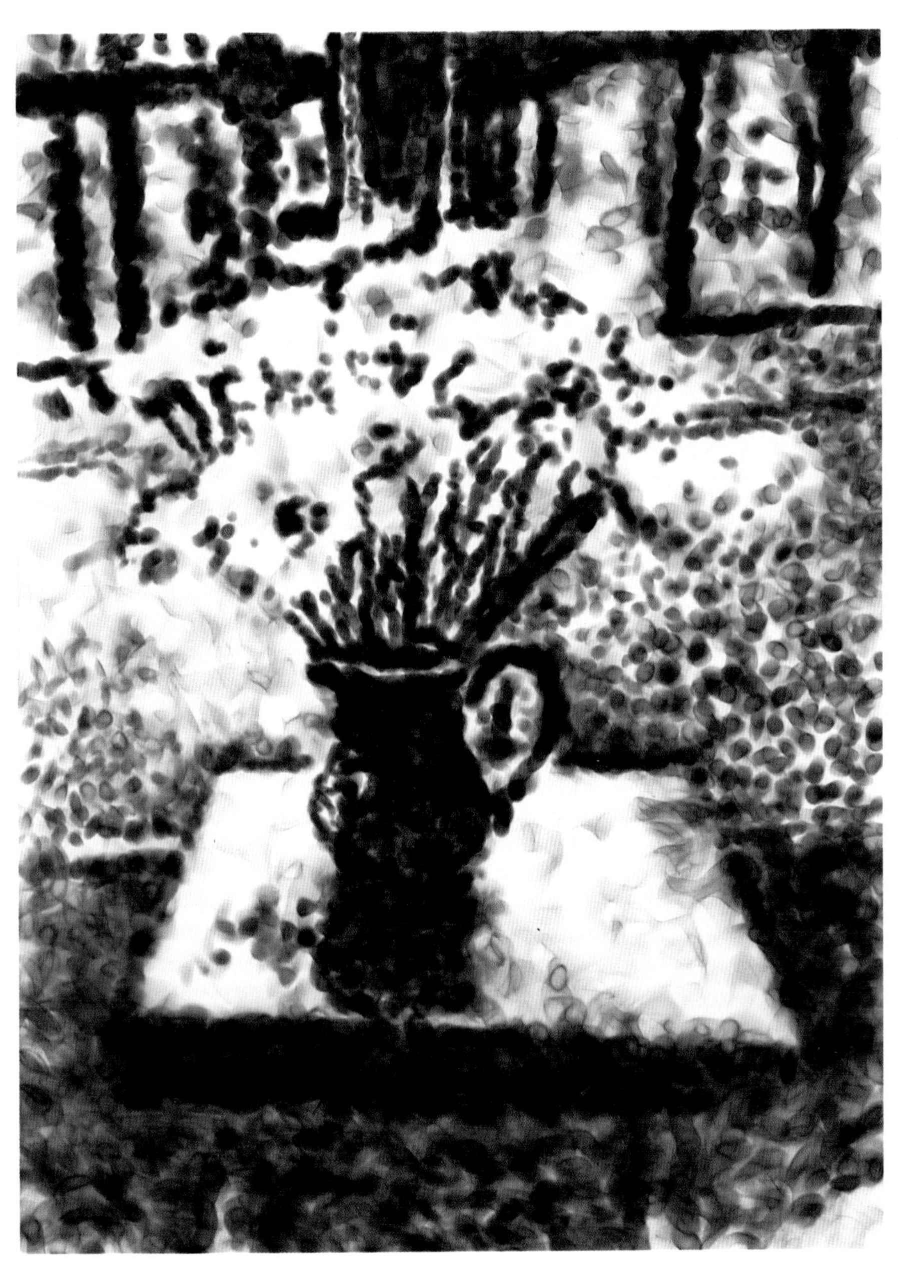

Subasta Yo Picasso, *78¾ × 86½", 200 × 220 cm., 1989*

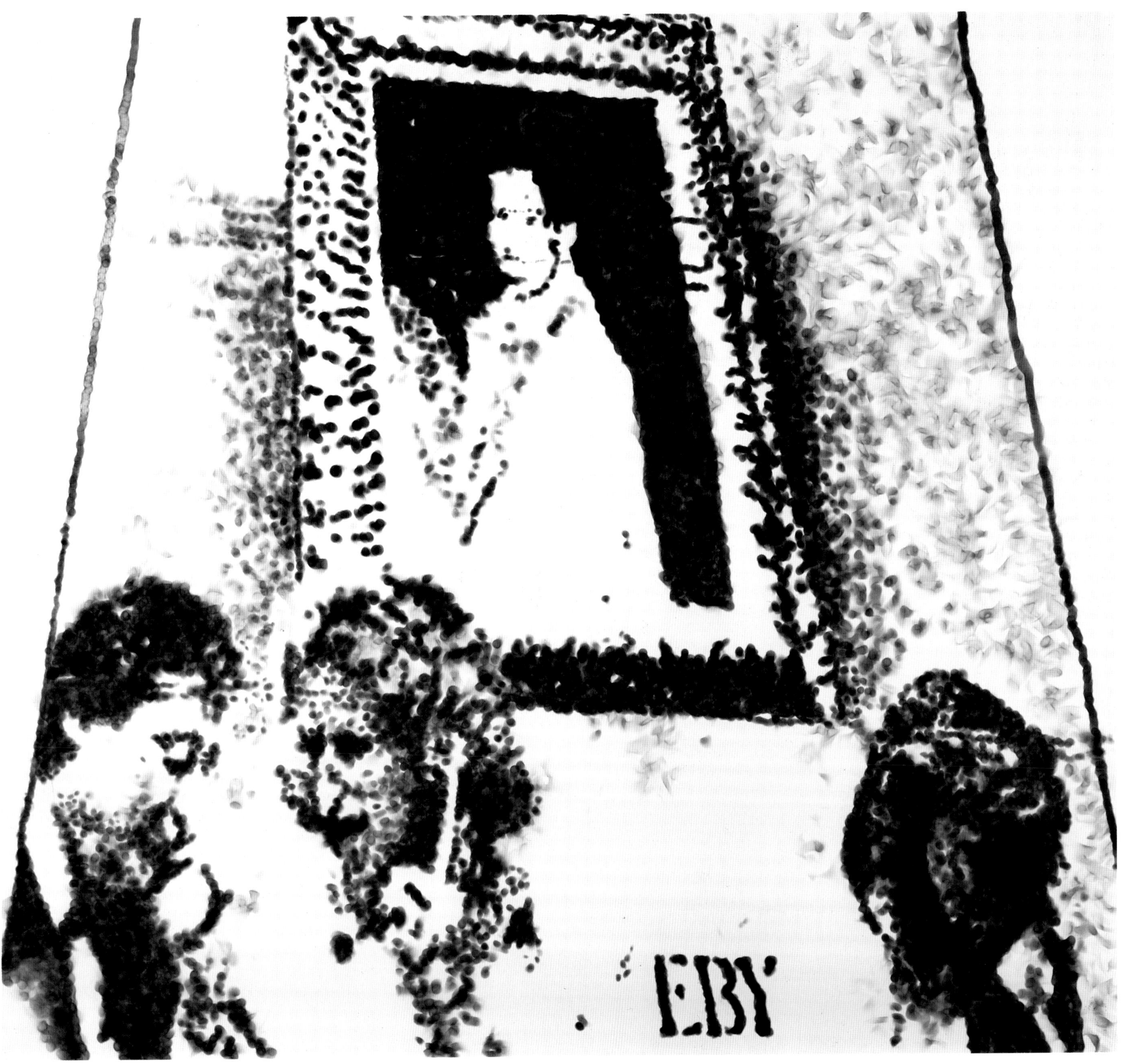
EBY

Flores sobre una mesa redonda, 39⅜ × 31¾", 100 × 81 cm., 1989

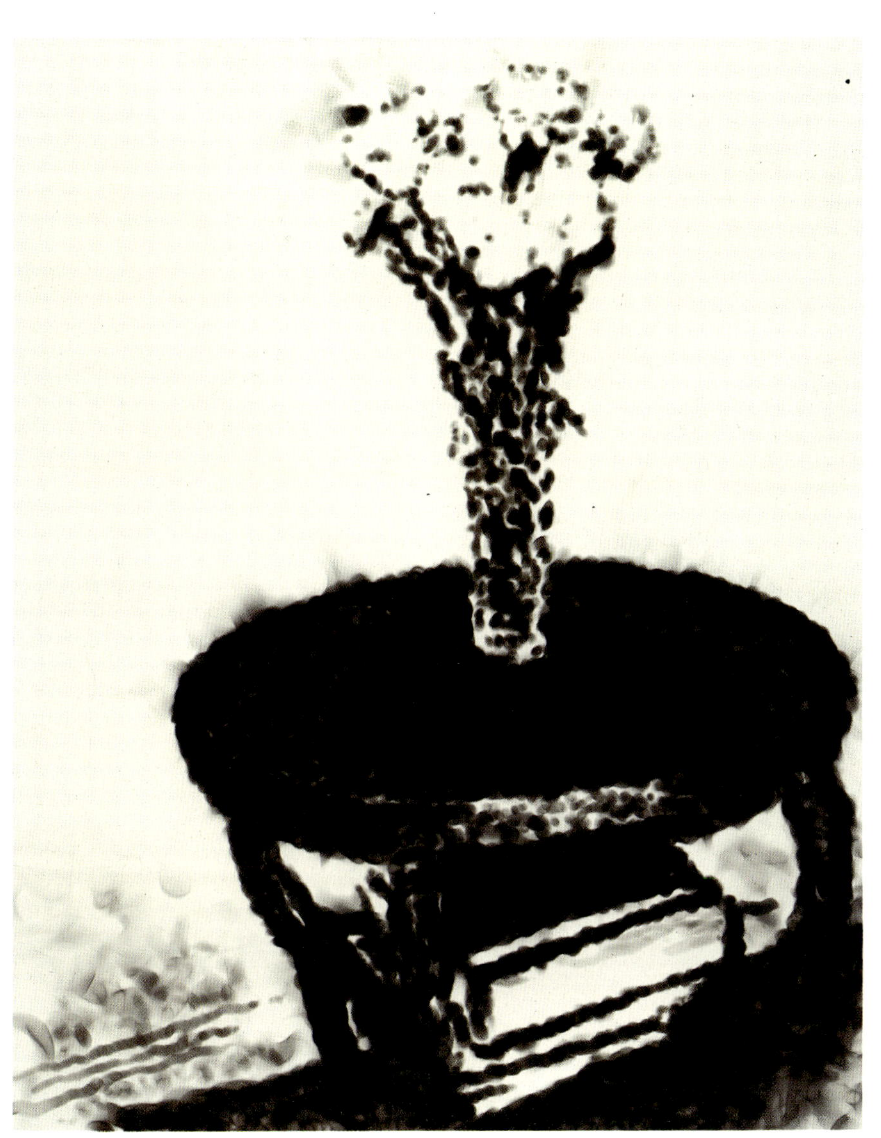

Subasta van Gogh, *98½ × 78¾", 250 × 200 cm., 1989*

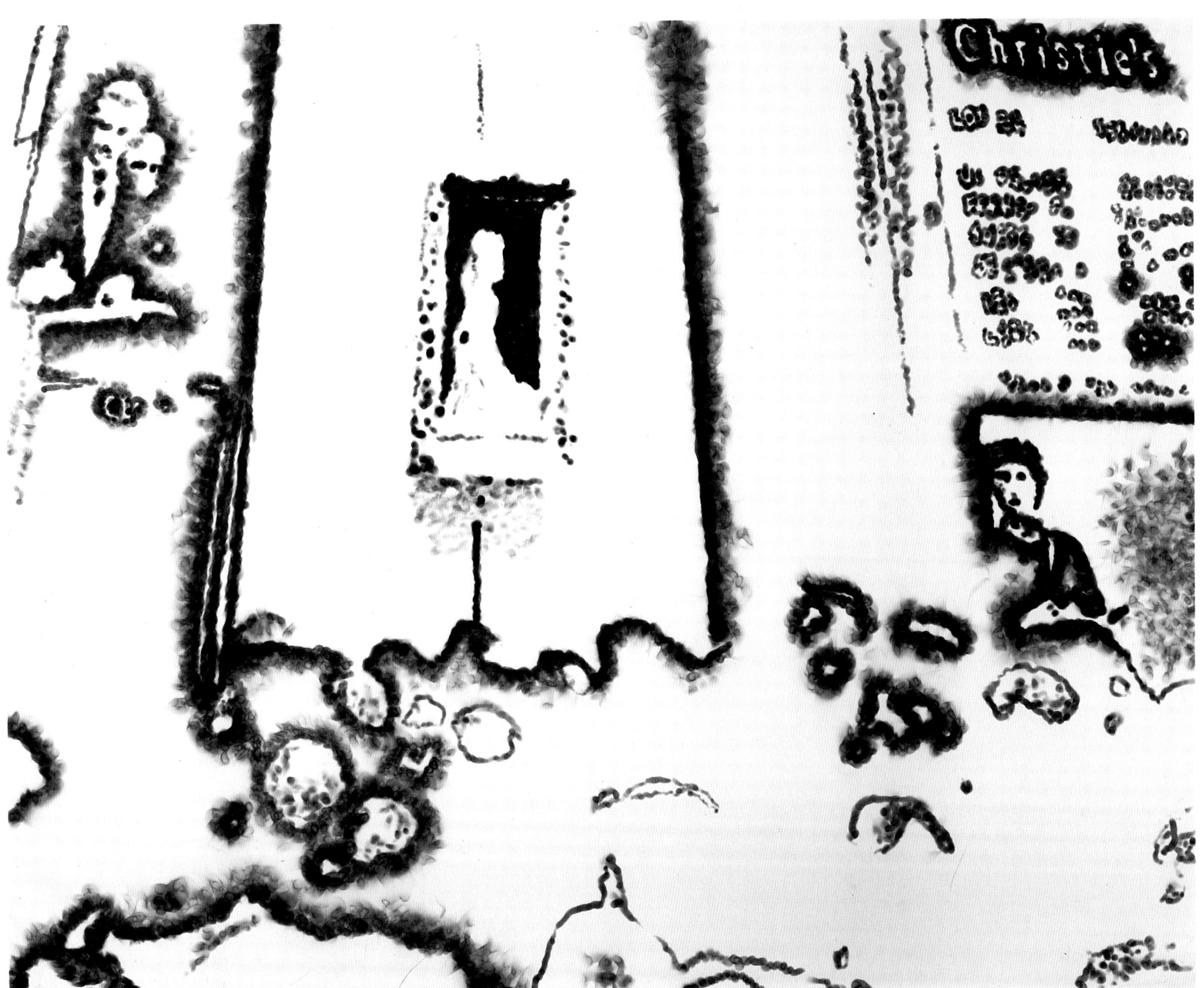

Christie's

Estrellas de mar y flores sobre un mesa, *39⅜ × 31¾″, 100 × 81 cm., 1989*

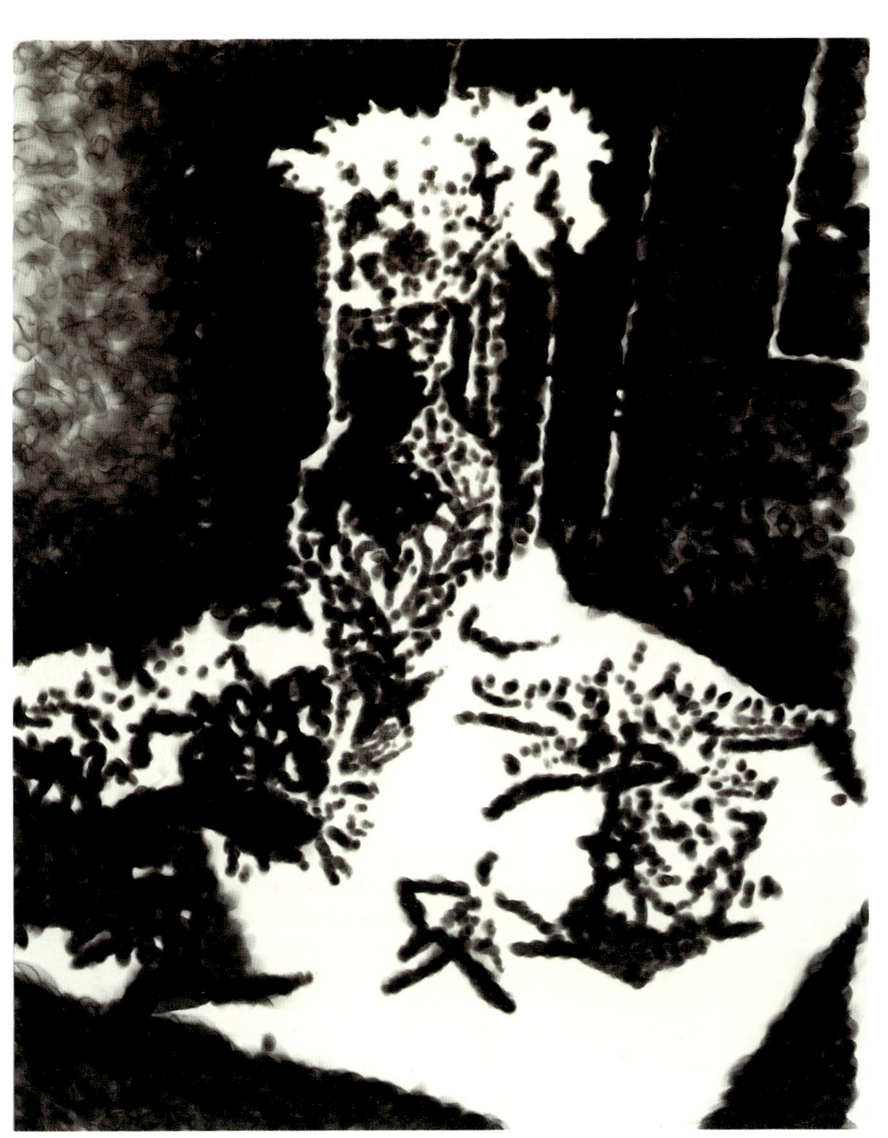

Auction at Christie's, *59×47¼", 150×120 cm., 1989*

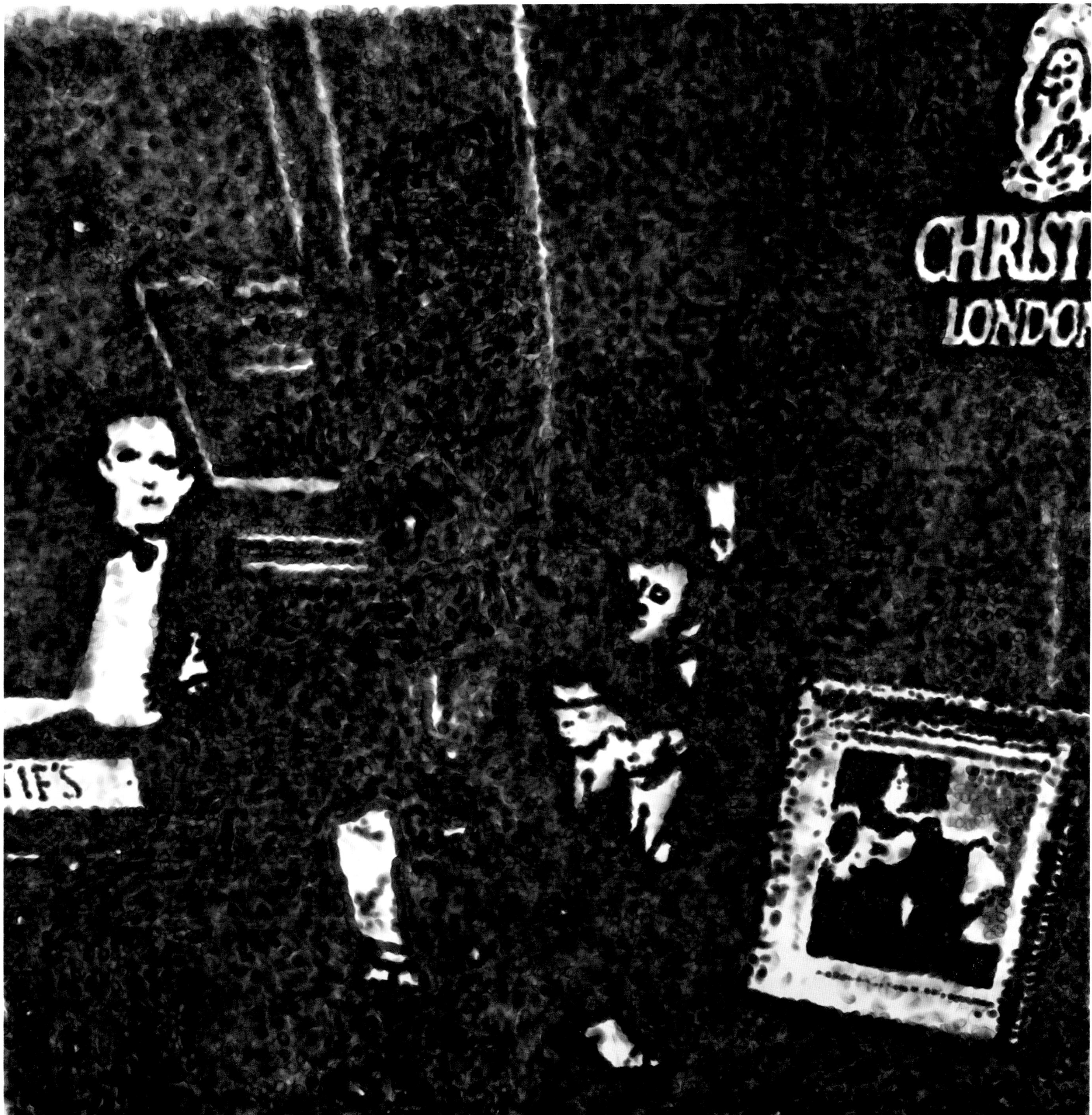
CHRISTI
LONDO
IE'S

Subasta van Gogh, *118¼ × 78¾″, 300 × 200 cm., 1989*

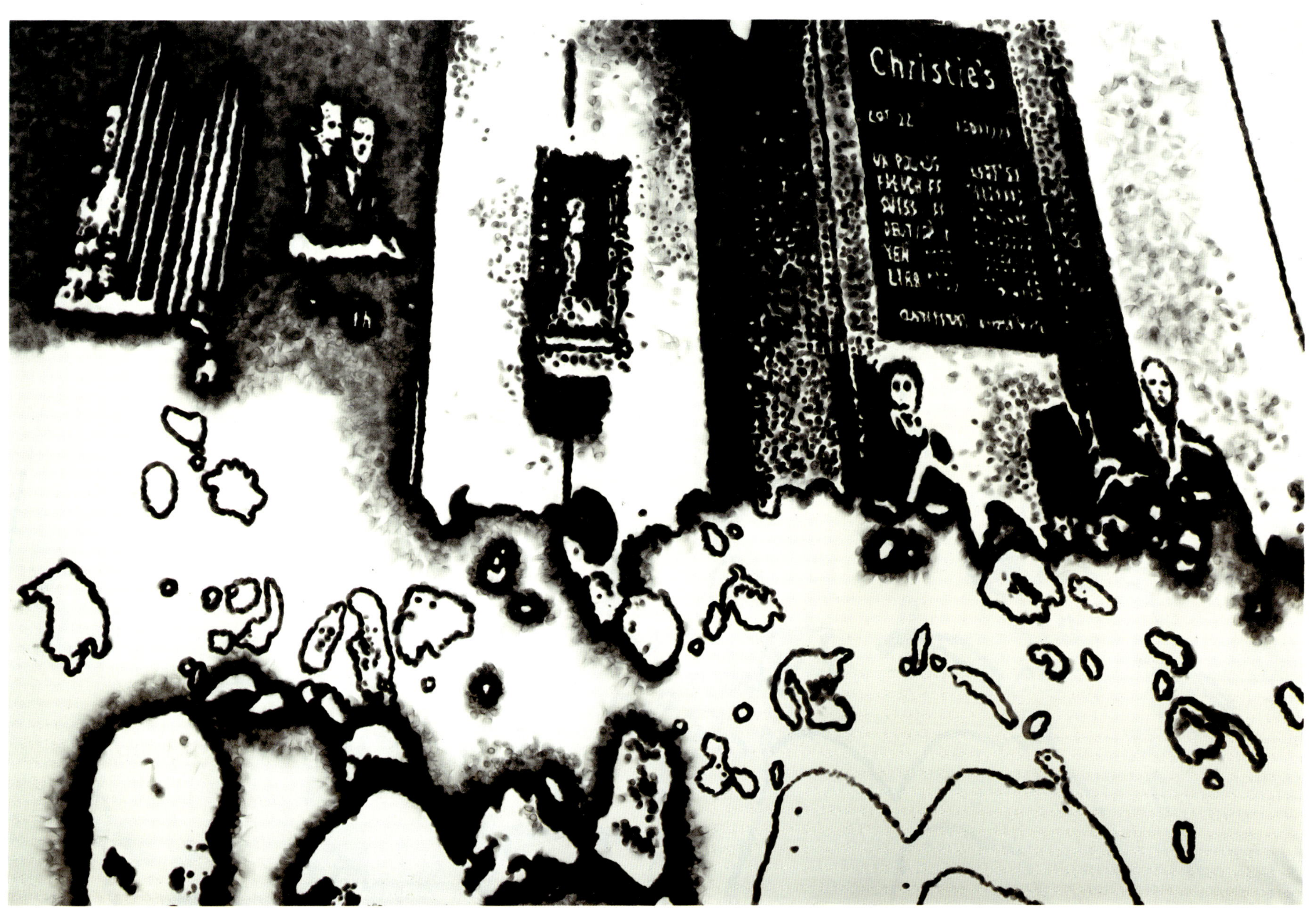

Christie's
LOT 22
YEN
LIRA

Flores sobre una silla, *39⅜ × 31¾", 100 × 81 cm., 1989*

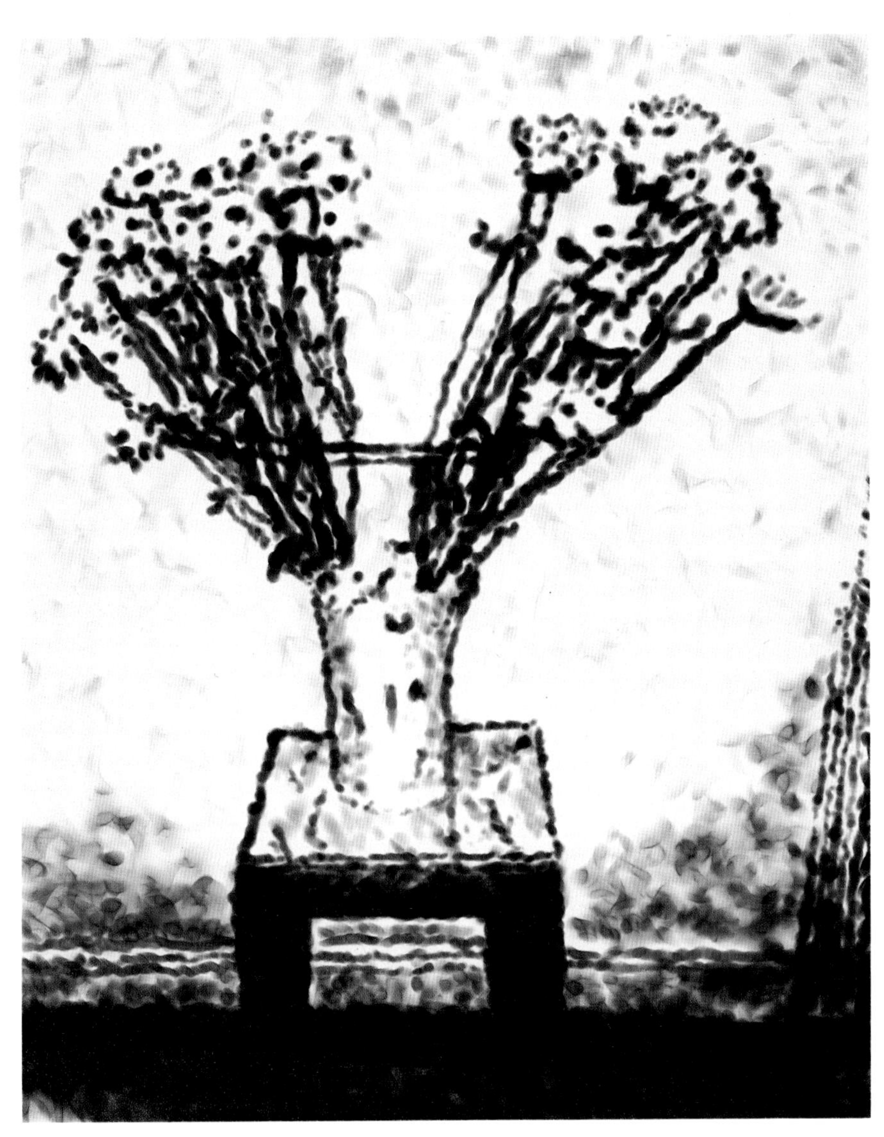

Subasta Sun Flowers, *118¼ × 78¾", 300 × 200 cm., 1989*

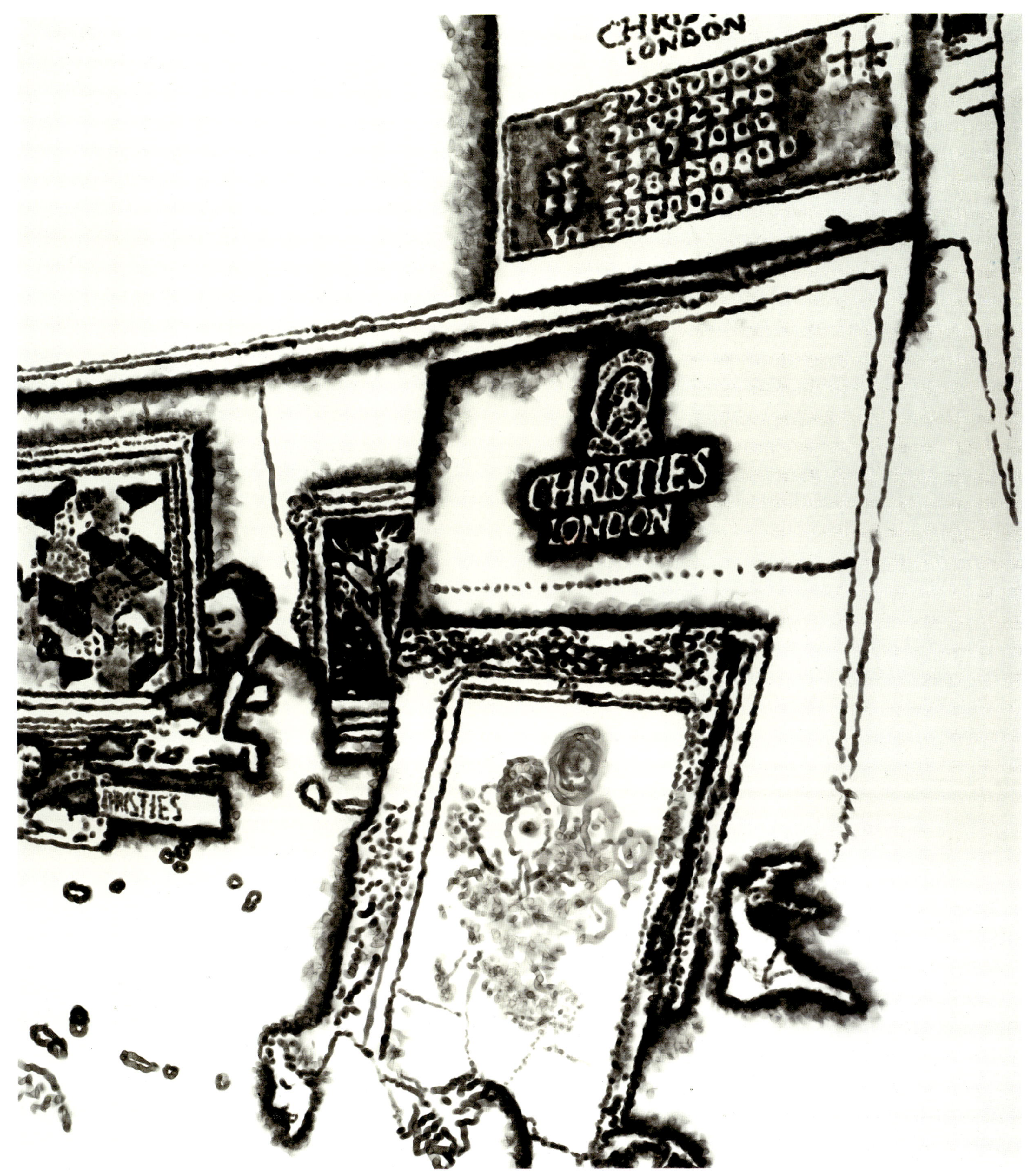

CHRISTIE'S
LONDON
CHRISTIES
LONDON
CHRISTIES

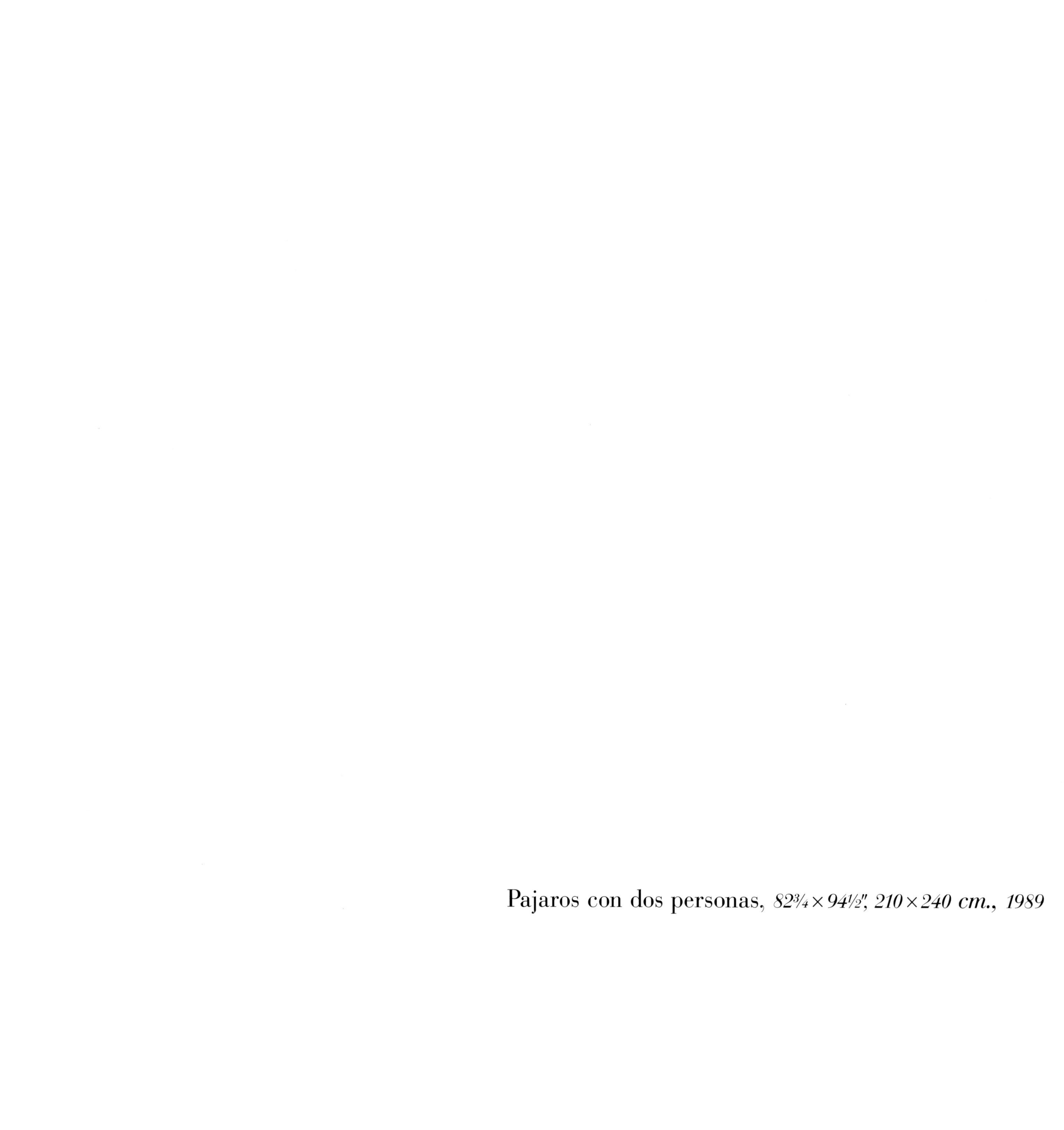

Pajaros con dos personas, *82¾×94½″, 210×240 cm., 1989*

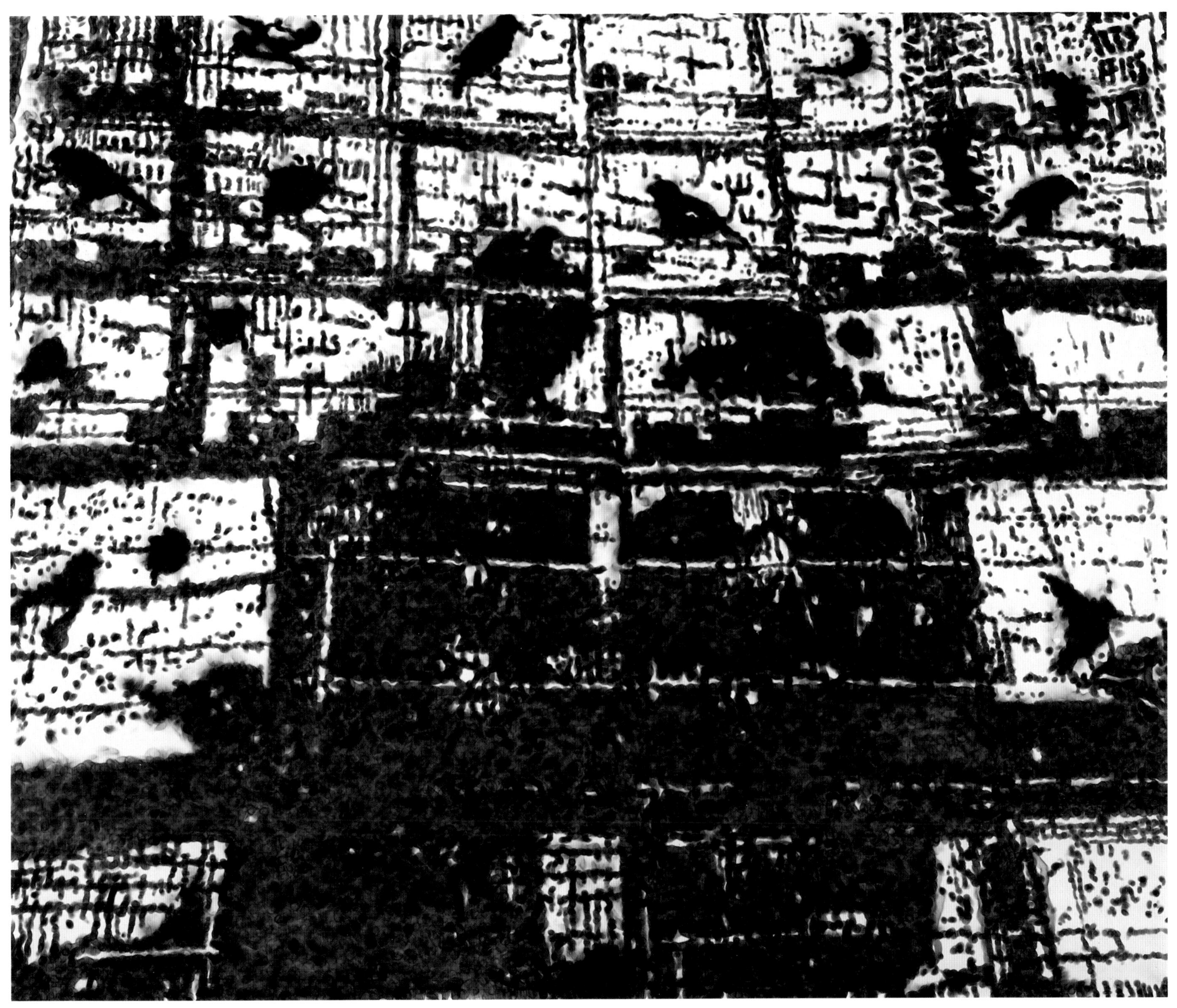

Lavado, *44¾×63¾", 114×162 cm., 1989*

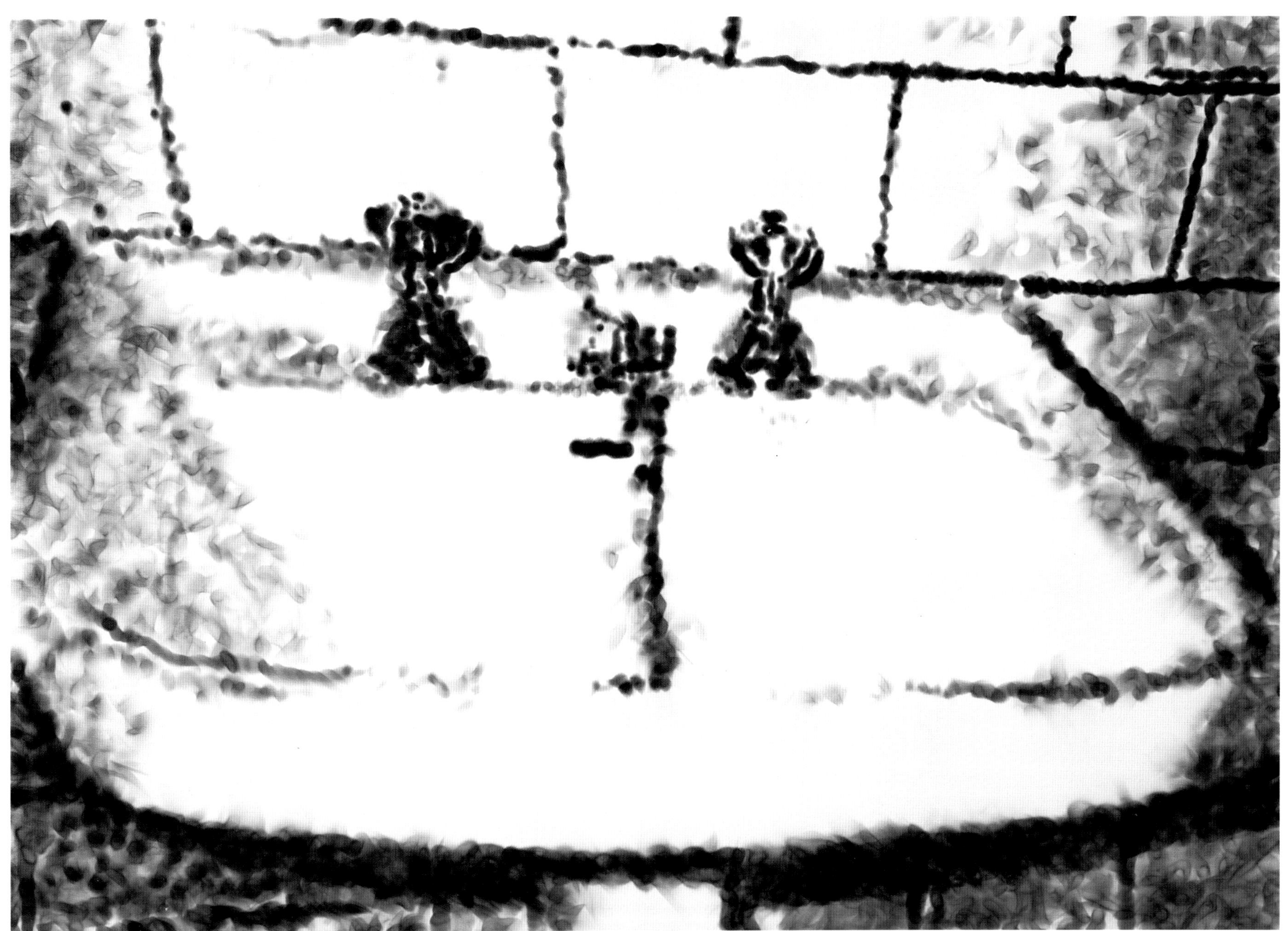

Woods, *51¼×63¾″, 130×162 cm., 1989*

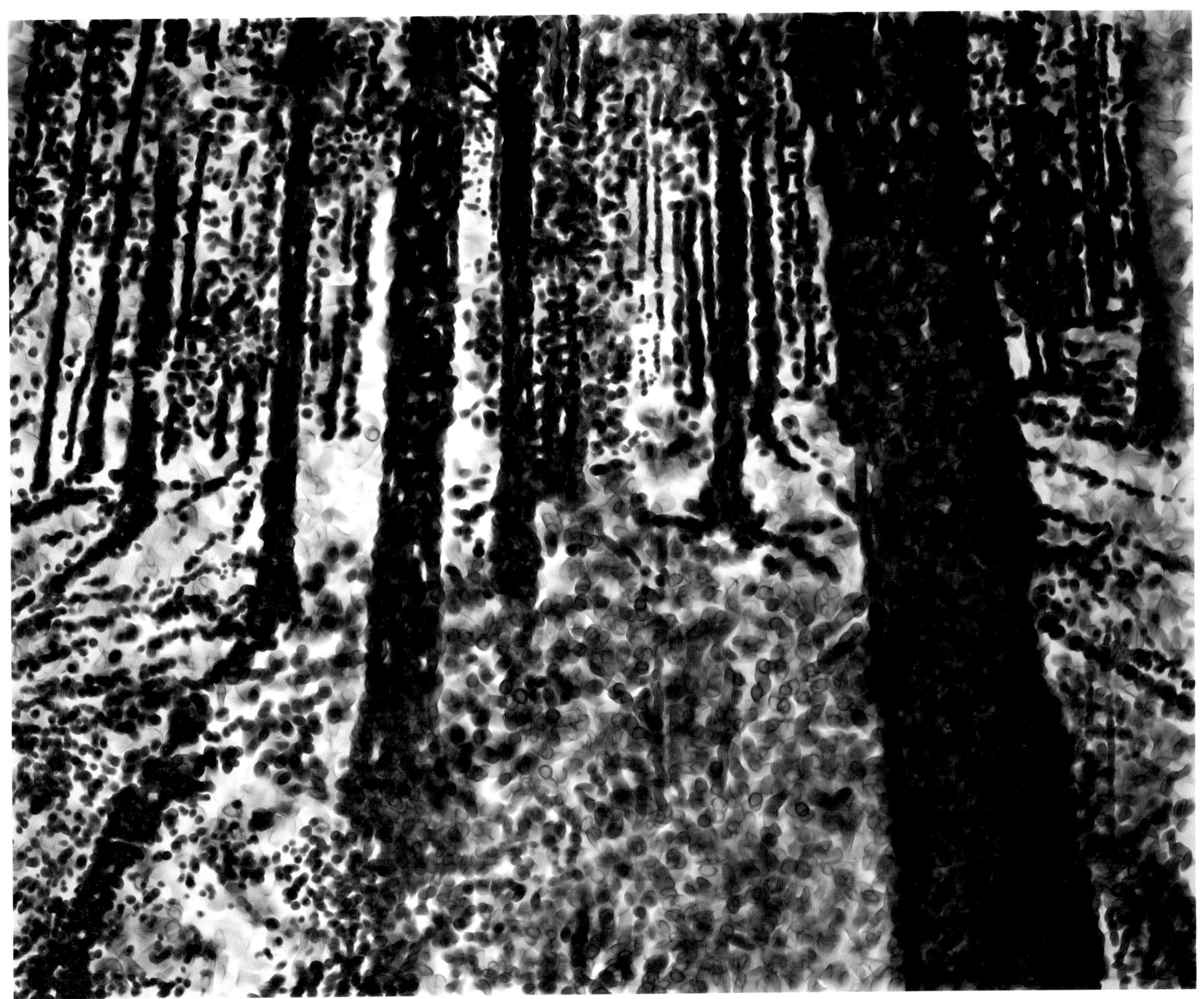

Trafic, 78¾ × 78¾", 200 × 200 cm., 1989

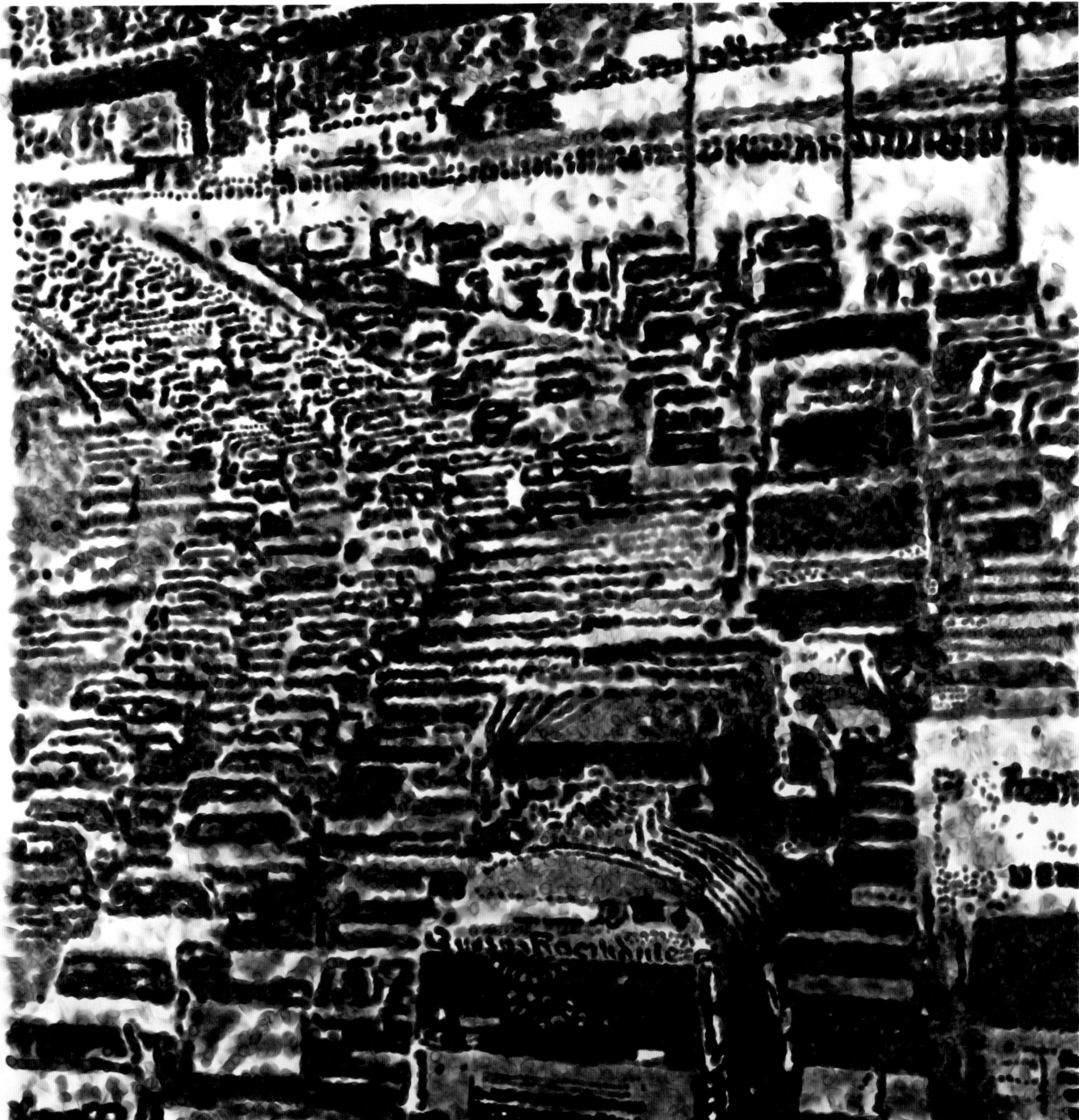

Jiri Georg Dokoupil

Born June 3, 1954 in Krnov, Czechoslavakia

EDUCATION

Art studies in Cologne, Frankfurt and at the Cooper Union, New York, with Hans Haacke, 1976–78

Guest teacher at the Kunstakademie Düsseldorf, 1983–84

Guest teacher at Circulo de bellas Artes, Madrid, 1989

Lives and works in Cologne, Teneriffe and Madrid

SOLO EXHIBITIONS

1982

Paul Maenz, Cologne, West Germany, "Jiri Georg Dokoupil: New Cologne School"

Galerie 't Venster, Rotterdam, The Netherlands, "Ein Pinsel" (collaborative paintings with Walter Dahn)

Chantal Crousel, Paris, France, "Jiri Georg Dokoupil"

Helen van der Meij, Amsterdam, The Netherlands, "Jiri Georg Dokoupil"

1983

Paul Maenz, Cologne, West Germany, "Portraits"

Six Friedrich, Munich, West Germany, "Jiri Georg Dokoupil"

Produzentengalerie Hamburg, Hamburg, West Germany, "Ricki: The Shower Paintings." Tour: Paul Maenz, Cologne, West Germany; Six Friedrich, Munich, West Germany (collaborative paintings with Walter Dahn)

Mary Boone Gallery, New York, "Jiri Georg Dokoupil"

Chantal Crousel, Paris, France, "Mixtura Dokoupiliana"

1984

Galerie Schurr, Stuttgart, West Germany, "Jiri Georg Dokoupil"

Groninger Museum, The Netherlands, "Shower and Africa Paintings" (collaborative paintings with Walter Dahn)

Paul Maenz, Cologne, West Germany, "Therapeutic Paintings"

Museum Folkwang, Essen, West Germany, "Dokoupil: Works from 1981–1984"

1985

Kunstmuseum Lucerne, Switzerland, "Dokoupil: Works from 1981–1984"

Crousel-Husenot, Paris, France, "Jiri Georg Dokoupil"

Galeria Leyendecker, Santa Cruz de Tenerife, Spain, "Jiri Georg Dokoupil"

Paul Maenz, Cologne, West Germany, "Mülheimer Freiheit-Neue wilde Paintings" (collaborative paintings with Walter Dahn)

Groninger Museum, The Netherlands, "Dokoupil: Works from 1981–1984"

Paul Maenz, Cologne, West Germany, "Corporations & Products"

Espace Lyonnais d'Art Contemporain, Lyon, France, "Dokoupil: Works from 1981–1984"

Vera Munro, Hamburg, West Germany (collaborative paintings with Walter Dahn)

Paule Anglim Gallery, San Francisco, "Jiri Georg Dokoupil"

Asher/Faure Gallery, Los Angeles, "Jiri Georg Dokoupil"

Heinrich Erhardt Gallerie, Frankfurt, West Germany, "Jiri Georg Dokoupil"

Leo Castelli, New York, "Jiri Georg Dokoupil"

1986

Galerie 121, Antwerp, Belgium, "Jiri Georg Dokoupil"

Galleria Marilena Bonomo, Bari, Italy, "Jiri Georg Dokoupil"

Ileana Sonnabend, New York, "Jiri Georg Dokoupil"

1987

Paul Maenz, Cologne, West Germany, "Religious Paintings"

Galleria Leyendecker, Santa Cruz de Tenerife, Spain, "Jiri Georg Dokoupil"

Six Friedrich, Munich, West Germany, "Jiri Georg Dokoupil"

Galerie Swart, Amsterdam, The Netherlands, "Drawings 1983–1987"

Galerie Dacic, Tübingen, West Germany, "Drawings 1987"

Galleria Marconi, Milan, Italy, "Jiri Georg Dokoupil"

Galerie Bischofberger, Zurich, Switzerland, "Zodiacs"

1988

Galeria Marilena Bonomo, Bari, Italy, "Jiri Georg Dokoupil"

Galeria Juana Aizpuru, Madrid, Spain, "Jiri Georg Dokoupil"

Galeria Juana Aizpuru, Sevilla, Spain, "Jiri Georg Dokoupil"

1989

Galerie Nikolaus Sonne, Berlin, West Germany, "Drawings"

Caja des Pensiones, Madrid, Spain, "Jiri Georg Dokoupil"

Galerie Massimo Minini, Brescia, Italy, "Drawings"

Galerie Ricky Swart, Amsterdam, The Netherlands "Drawings"

Galerie Leyendecker, Santa Cruz de Tenerife, Spain, "Jiri Georg
Dokoupil"
Galerie Beaubourg, Paris, France, "Jiri Georg Dokoupil"
Robert Miller Gallery, New York, "Jiri Georg Dokoupil"

GROUP EXHIBITIONS

1980
Hahnentorburg, Cologne, West Germany, "Auch wenn das Perlhuhn
leise weint" (with H.P. Adamski, P. Bommels, W. Dahn)

1981
Groninger Museum, The Netherlands, "New German Art I—
Mülheimer Freiheit"
Lothringer Str. 13, Munich, West Germany, "German Overview I"
Im Klapperhof 33, Cologne, West Germany, German Overview II"
Paul Maenz, Cologne, West Germany, "Der grüne Hühnerficker ist
endlich traurig" (with H.P. Adamski, P. Bommels, W. Dahn, G.
Kever, G. Naschberger)
Akademie der Künste, Berlin, West Germany, "Image Exchange:
New Painting from Germany"
Kunstverein Freiburg, West Germany, "The Secret Truth: Mulheimer
Freiheit"
Alte Oper, Frankfurt, West Germany, "Phoenix"
Paul Maenz, Cologne, West Germany, "Lust of the Flesh: The Return
of Sensuality—Eroticism in New Art"
Kunsthalle Wilhelmshaven, West Germany; Kunstverein Wolfsburg,
West Germany, "The Sea-Voyage and Death—Mülheimer Freiheit,"
(1982)

1982
Museum Folkwang, Essen, West Germany, "Ten Artists from
Germany"
Kunsthalle Basel, Switzerland; Museum Boymans-van Beuningen,
Rotterdam, The Netherlands, "Twelve Artists from Germany"
Kassel, West Germany, "Documenta 7"
Berlin, West Germany, "Zeitgeist"
Venice, Italy, "Biennale"
Ulmer Museum, "Tendencies 82"
Galerie 121, Antwerp, Belgium
Schranne, Laupheim
Galerie Swart, Amsterdam, "Drawings"
Galerie nächst St. Stephan, Vienna, Austria, "Group Show"
Klapperhof, Cologne, West Germany, "The New Artist Group: The
Wild Painters" (with W. Dahn and A.Schulze)

Gallery of Modern Art, Bologna, Italy, "Young Painting in Germany"
(organization Zdenek Felix)
Six Friedrich, Munich, West Germany, "Five From Cologne"

1983
Museum am Ostwall, Dortmund, West Germany, "Expressionism—
'Neue Wilde' "
The Scottish Arts Council, Edinburgh; Institute of Contemporary Art,
London, "Mülheimer Freiheit Proudly Presents the Second
Bombing" (1984)
Museum Folkwang, Essen, West Germany, "Works from the FER
Collection" (1984)

1984
Galerie Krinzinger, Innsbruck, Austria; Museum Villa Stuck,
Munich, West Germany; Rheinisches Landesmuseum Bonn, West
Germany, "Taking Stock: New German Painting"
Barcelona, Madrid, Spain, "Origin and Vision: New German
Painting"
Museum of Modern Art, New York, "An International Survey of
Recent Painting and Sculpture"
Barbara Farber, Amsterdam, The Netherlands, "The European
Attack" (Drawings)
Bonner Kunstverein; Kunstmuseum Bonn, West Germany, "Take
DaDa Seriously—It's Worth It!"
Galerie 121, Antwerp, Belgium, "Drawings"
Galerie Barbara J.-Jandrig, Krefeld, West Germany
Stadt Gelsenkirchen, West Germany, "Paul Maenz Presents: Six Neue
Wilde"
Barbara Gladstone Gallery, New York, "Drawings"
Dublin, Ireland, "ROSC"
Kitakyushu Municipal Museum of Art, Japan, "Painting Now"
Kunsthalle Tübingen, West Germany, "7,000 Oaks"
Galerie Philomene Magers, Bonn, West Germany, "Ping-Pong"
Düsseldorf, West Germany, "von hier aus"
Paul Maenz, Cologne, West Germany, "Sechs Richtige"
Kasseler Kunstverein, Kassel, West Germany, "Watercolors"
Cultural Development Center, Bologne-sur-Mer, France,
"COLOGNE…Nouveaux Regards"
National Institute of Arts, Mexico, "Origin and Vision—New German
Painting" (collaborative paintings with Walter Dahn, to 2/10/85)
Monika Spruth Galerie, Cologne, West Germany, "Nouveaux
Bohéme"

1985

Turin, Italy, "Rheingold"

Paris, France, "XIIIe Biennale de Paris"

Amsterdam, The Netherlands, Kunst RAI

Bologna, Italy, "Anniottanta"

Sao Paulo, Brasil, "18. Biennale"

Municipal Gallery, Saarbrücken, West Germany

Graz, Austria, Styrian Autumn

Museum of Art, Carnegie Institute, Pittsburgh, "Carnegie
International"

Galleria Leyendecker, Santa Cruz de Tenerife, Spain, "Mixed Pickles"

Wilhelm-Hack-Museum, Ludwigshafen, West Germany,
"Apocalypse—A Principle of Hope"

National Gallery, Berlin, West Germany, "1945–1985: Art in the
Federal Republic"

Frankfurter Kunstverein, Frankfurt, West Germany, "Of Drawing—
Aspects of Drawing"

Provincial Museum, Hasselt, The Netherlands, "New German
Painting from The Ludwig Collection"

Galerie Holtmann, Cologne, West Germany, "Cologne in Black
and White"

Galerie Barbara Farber, Amsterdam, The Netherlands, "Master
Works on Paper"

1986

Gimpel Fils, London, England, "Between Identity/Politics A New
Art"

Art Gallery of South Australia, Adelaide; Art Gallery of Western
Australia, Perth; National Art Gallery, Wellington, "Wild Visionary
Spectral—New German Art"

Metternich House, Koblenz, West Germany, "New German Art from
The Ludwig Collection"

Sydney, Australia, "Biennale"

Center for Knowledge, Bonn, West Germany, "The Other Glance:
Healing Effects of Art Today" (collaborative paintings with
Walter Dahn)

Louisiana Museum, Humlebaek, Denmark, "The Global Dialogue"

Arnheim, The Netherlands, "Sonsbeek 86"

Galerie Varisella, Nuremberg, West Germany, "Sunrise"

Städt Galerie im Lenbachhaus, Munich, West Germany, "In Honor
of Beuys"

Frankfurter Kunstverein, Frankfurt, West Germany, "Prospect 86"

Tony Shafrazi Gallery, New York, "What It Is"

Galerie Arnesen, Copenhagen, Denmark "Dahn/Dokoupil/Schulze"

Galleria Schipke, Sofia, Bulgaria, "Sie machen was Sie wollen"

1987

Galerie und Edition Karl Pfefferle, Munich, West Germany, "Painting
in Europe, Positions/Part I"

Palais des Beaux-Arts, Charleroi, France, "Exoticism of the
Everyday"

Museum of Contemporary Art, Sevilla, Spain, "Sie machen was
Sie wollen"

Mannheimer Kunstverein, "Sculpture by Painters"

Los Angeles County Museum of Art, Los Angeles, "Avant-Garde in
the Eighties"

Lagos, Nigeria, Goethe Institute (with Walter Dahn and Twins 77)

Century 87, Amsterdam, The Netherlands, "La vie en rose" (with
Rob Scholte)

Galerie Daniel Buchholz, Cologne, West Germany, "Multiples"

Museum van Bommel, Venlo, "Sculpture by Painters"

Galerie Sonne, Berlin, West Germany, "Images of Man"

Yvon Lambert, Paris, France, "Art Against AIDS"

Strassbourg, "Eighty—The Painters of Europe"

Centro de Arte Reina Sofia, Madrid, Spain, "Collection Sonnabend"

1988

Galerie Hufkens-Noirhomme, Brussels, Belgium, "A Thick Layer
Underfoot"

Galerie Bonomi, Rome, Italy, collaborative exhibition with Rob
Scholte and Peter Schuyff

Metro Pictures, New York, "Group Show"

Michael Kohn Gallery, Los Angeles, "Group Show"

Vrej Baghoomian, Inc., New York, "Summer Exhibition"

Museo d'Arte Contemporanea, Prato, Italy, "Europe Now"

National Museum of Contemporary Art, Seoul, South Korea,
"Olympiad of Art"

Dumont-Kunsthalle, Cologne, West Germany, "Made in Cologne"

Kunsthaus Hamburg, Hamburg, West Germany, "Work in History—
History in Work"

Museum van Hedendaagse Kunst, Antwerp, Belgium, "Gran Pavese:
The Flag-Project"

Galerie Paul Maenz, Cologne, West Germany, "Museums & Banks—
Nine Bronzes" (with Peter Roehr)

Kölnischer Kunstverein, Cologne, West Germany, "F. C. Gundlach
Collection, Hamburg"

Bonnefantenmuseum in Maastricht, The Netherlands, "The
Postmodern Explained to Children"

Galerie Juana de Aizpuru, Madrid and Sevilla, Spain, "Group Show"

Museo Municipal de bellas Artes, Santa Cruz de Tenerife, Spain, "An

Hour Before" (group show with Mark Dagley, Walter Dahn, Salvo
and Andreas Schulze)
Cologne, West Germany, Auction for the National AIDS Foundation,
"Art Against AIDS"
Toledo Museum of Art, Toledo, Spain; Guggenheim Museum, New
York; Williamstown Museum of Art, Williamstown, Kunstmuseum-
Dusseldorf, West Germany; Schirn-Kunsthalle, Frankfurt, West
Germany, "Refigured Painting: The German Image 1960–1988"
Pontevedra-Galicia, Spain, "Bienal—International de Arte"

1989
Horsens Kunstmuseum, Lunden, Denmark, "Art from Cologne"
Galerie Leyendecker, Santa Cruz de Tenerife, Spain, "Looking
and Learning"
Santa Cruz De Tenerife; Museo Municipal de bellas Artes; Centro
de Arte la Regenta; Las Palmas de Gran Canaria, Spain, "An
Hour Before"
Galerie Kaess-Weiss, Stuttgart, West Germany, "Drawings"
Galerie Nikolaus Sonne, Berlin, West Germany, "Carpets"
Kunstverein Hamburg, West Germany, "F. C. Gundlach Collection,
Hamburg"
Museum van Hedendaagse Kunst, Gent, Belgium, "Open Mind"
Museum des 20. Jahrhunderts, Vienna, Austria, "Viennese Divan"
La Gomera, Spain, "Studio of the South"

<h1 style="text-align:center">Jiri Georg Dokoupil – Selected Bibliography</h1>

ARTICLES

Haks, Frans and Faust, Wolfgang Max, "Nieuwe Duitse Kunst I: Mülheimer Freiheit," Groninger Museum, exhibition catalogue, 1981

Busche, Ernst; Schwarz, Michael and Kneif, Tibor, "Bildwechsel-Neue Malerei aus Deutschland," Art Academy of Berlin, exhibition catalogue, 1981

"Die heimliche Wahrheit – Mülheimer Freiheit," Kunstverein Freiburg, exhibition catalogue, 1981

Iden, Peter, *Das Kunstwerk* 6 XXXIV, 1981, "Die Hochgemuten Nichtskönner"

Nemeczek, Alfred, *Art*, October 1981, "Die Sache mit den Wilden"

Kusak, A., *Stern*, Nr. 41, October 1981, "Die Neue Malwut"

"Die Seefahrt und der Tod – Mülheimer Freiheit," Kunsthalle Wilhelmshaven; Kunstverein Wolfsburg, exhibition catalogue, 1981–82

Faust, Wolfgang Max, *Kunstforum International*, December 1981–January 1982, "Deutsche Kunst, hier, heute"

Faust, Wolfgang Max, *Art Forum*, No. 106, December 1981–January 1982, "Mülheimer Freiheit"

Hohmeyer, Jurgen, *Der Spiegel*, Nr. 22, 36. Jahrgang, May 82, "Sturmflut der Bilder"

Faust, Wolfgang Max and de Vries, Gerd, "Hunger nach Bildern – Deutsche Malerei der Gegenwart," DuMont Buchverlag, Cologne, 1982

"10 Künstler aus Deutschland," Kunsthalle Basel; Museum Boymans-van Beuningen, Rotterdam, exhibition catalogue, 1982

"12 Künstler aus Deutschland," Kunsthalle Basel; Museum Boymans-van Beuningen, Rotterdam, exhibition catalogue, 1982

"Documenta 7," Kassel, exhibition catalogue, 1982

"Zeitgeist," Berlin, exhibition catalogue, 1982

Kuspit, Donald B., *Art in America*, September 1982, "Europe 82 – Acts of Aggression: German Painting Today"

Simmen, Jeannot L., *Flash Art International*, No. 109, November 1982, "New Painting in Germany"

"Tendenzen 82," Ulmer Museum, exhibition catalogue, 1982

"La giovane pittura in Germania," Galleria d'arte moderna, Bologna, exhibition catalogue, 1982

Crone, Rainer, *Artforum*, March 1983, "Jiri Georg Dokoupil: The Imprisoned Brain"

Sauer, Christel, (Hrsg. Paul Maenz), "Die Sammlung FER – The Fer Collection," Cologne, 1983

"Mülheimer Freiheit Proudly Presents The Second Bombing," The Scottish Arts Council, Edinburgh; Institute of contemporary Art, London, exhibition catalogue, 1983–1984

Dickhoff, Wilfried W., Interview with Jiri Georg Dokoupil, *Wolkenkratzer*, November–December 1983, "Das letze Abenteuer der Menschheit"

Faust, Wolfgang Max, *Kunstforum International*, Vol. 67, November 11, 1983, "Gemeinschaftsbilder – Ein Aspekt der neuen Malerei"

Honnef, Klaus, *Kunstforum International*, Vol. 68, December 12, 1983, "Zwischenbilanz II – Neue Deutsche Malerei"

van Damme, Leo, *Arte Factum*, February 1984, "The Modernist Reaction: The Unilateral Misunderstanding"

Spazio Humano, 1984, No. 2

Grasskamp, Walter, Interview with Jiri Georg Dokoupil, "Origin and Vision: New German Painting," Ministry of Culture, Madrid, Spain, exhibition catalogue, 1984

Simmen, Jeannot L., *Flash Art International*, No. 118, Summer 1984, "Paraphrases or Key Pictures"

Ottmann, Klaus, *Flash Art International*, No. 118, Summer 1984, "MOMA: An International Survey – Wake Up Kynaston McShine"

Levin, Kim, *Flash Art International*, No. 118, Summer 1984, "MOMA: An International Survey – What An Eye!"

Beyer, Lucie, *Flash Art International*, No. 118, Summer 1984, "Jiri Georg Dokoupil at Galerie Schurr, Stuttgart"

Hecht, Axel, Interview with Jiri Georg Dokoupil, *Art*, August 1984

"ROSC – A Poetry of Vision," Dublin, Ireland, exhibition catalogue, 1984

Flash Art International, No. 120, January 1985, "Jiri Georg Dokoupil – Two Letters from the Artist's Mother"

Schmidt-Wulffen, Stephan, *Flash Art International*, No. 120, January 1985, "Georg Dokoupil – Folkwang Museum Essen, Maenz, Cologne"

Dokoupil, Jiri Georg, *Spazio Humano*, Nr. 2, April–June 1985

Taylor, Paul, *Interview Magazine*, October 1985, "Sturm und Trash – Jiri Georg Dokoupil"

Leccese, Pasquale, *Juliet Art Magazine*, No. 22, October– November 1985

"Tiefe Blicke – Kunst der achtziger Jahre," DuMont Buchverlag 1985

"1945–1985: Kunst in der Bundesrepublik," Nationalgalerie Berlin, exhibition catalogue, 1985

Murken-Altrogge, Christa and Murken, Axel-Hinrich, "Vom Expressionismus bis zur Soul and Body Art," DuMont Buchverlag 1985

Kuspit, Donald, *Artscribe*, December 1985–January 1986, "Jiri Georg Dokoupil at Leo Castelli"

Paltzer, Rolf A., *Art*, Nr. 1, January 1986, "Neue Aktualität des Porträts"

Grasskamp, Walter, *Flash Art International*, Nr. 125, December 1985–January 1986, "Disgusting Techniques"

Hapgood, Susan, *Flash Art International*, Nr. 125, December 1985–January 1986, "Jiri Georg Dokoupil at Leo Castelli"

Ottmann, Klaus, *Flash Art International*, Nr. 125, December 1985–January 1986, "The World According to Byars, Beuys, Dokoupil"

Schmidt-Wulffen, Stephan, *Noema*, Nr. 5, 1986, "Marke: Dokoupil 'Corporations & Products' und andere Neuigkeiten von Jiri Georg Dokoupil"

Alessandri, Giulio, *Flash Art*, Italian Edition, No. 129, November 1985, "Della deboleza della critica"

Grasskamp, Walter, *Flash Art*, French Edition, No. 10, March 1986, "Dokoupil at Maenz"

Maenz, Paul, *Flash Art*, French Edition, No. 10, March 1986, "Dokoupil et Maenz"

Di Pietrantonio, Giacinto, *Flash Art*, French Edition, No. 10, March 1986, "Le spectacle de l'art"

Becker, Wolfgang, "New German Art from The Ludwig Collection, Aachen," exhibition catalogue, 1986

"Wild Visionary Spectral: New German Art," Art Gallery of South Australia, Adelaide, exhibition catalogue, 1986

"Der andere Blick," DuMont exhibition catalogue, 1986

"Origins Originality & Beyond," Biennale, Sydney, exhibition catalogue, 1986

"Prospect 86," Frankfurter Kunstverein, exhibition catalogue, 1986

"What It Is," exhibition catalogue, Tony Shafrazi Gallery, New York, 1986

Grasskamp, Walter, "Der vergessliche Engel," Verlag Silke Schreiber, 1986

"Sonsbeek 86," Sonsbeek, Arnheim, exhibition catalogue, 1986

Godfrey, Tony, "The New Image: Paintings in the Eighties," 1986

"L'exotism au quótidien," Palais des Beaux-Artes, Charleroi, exhibition catalogue, 1987

Benzakin, Joel, *Des Artes*, "Les constructions du Banal," April 1987

Marcade, Bernard, *Art-press*, "Inventeur sans trade-mark," January 1987

"Avant-garde in the Eighties," Los Angeles County Museum of Art, Los Angeles, exhibition catalogue, 1987

Schmidt-Wulffen, Stephan, "Spielregeln-Tendenzen der Gegenwartskunst," DuMont Buchverlag, 1987

Spazio Humano, No. 1, 1987

Schwabsky, Barry, *Flash Art International*, No. 137, November–December 1987, "Jiri Georg Dokoupil: Spotlight"

La Luna, "Jiri Georg Dokoupil," No. 43, October 1987, Madrid, Spain

Väth-Hinz, Dr. Henriette, *Pan*, "Bilder wie vom Zeitgeist gemalt," No. 11, 1987

Kontova, Helena and Magnani, Gregorio, *Flash Art International*, Italian Edition, No. 142, January–February 1988. Interview with Jiri Georg Dokoupil

Honnef, Klaus, "Kunst der Gegenwart, 1988," Taschen Verlag

Fundacion Caja de Pensiones, Madrid, "Dokoupil," exhibition catalogue, text by Francisco Rivas

Bourriaud, Nicolas, *Flash Art*, No. 146, May–June 1989

PUBLICATIONS

"Jiri Georg Dokoupil: Neue Kölner Schule," Paul Maenz Gallery, Cologne, West Germany, 1982

"Ricki: The Shower Paintings," collaborative paintings by Walter Dahn and Jiri GeorgDokoupil, Paul Maenz Gallery, Cologne, 1983

"The Africa Paintings," collaborative paintings by Walter Dahn and Jiri Georg Dokoupil, Groninger Museum, The Netherlands, 1984

"Dokoupil: Works from 1981–1984," Museum Folkwang, Essen, West Germany, 1984

"Dokoupil: Corporations & Products," exhibition catalogue, Paul Maenz Gallery, Cologne, 1985

"Jiri Georg Dokoupil," exhibition catalogue, Biennale, Sao Paulo, Brasil, 1985

"Jiri Georg Dokoupil," Ernst A. Busche and Paul Maenz, Cologne, 1987

"Dokoupil," exhibition catalogue, Paul Maenz Gallery, Cologne; Galeria Leyendecker, Santa Cruz de Tenerife, Spain, 1987

"Dokoupil Drawings," Vol. I, in collaboration with Massimo Minini, Brescia, Italy

"Dokoupil Drawings," Vol. II, in collaboration with Nikolaus Sonne, Berlin, 1989

"Jiri Georg Dokoupil," Series 1982–1987, exhibition catalogue, Fundacion Caja de Pensiones, Madrid, 1989

"Dokoupil Drawings," Vol. III, in collaboration with Galeria Leyendecker, Santa Cruz de Tenerife, Spain, 1989

Van Abbemuseum, Eindhoven, The Netherlands
Neue Galerie, The Ludwig Collection, Aachen, West Germany
Groninger Museum, The Netherlands
Staatsgalerie, Stuttgart, West Germany
Museum Boymans van Beuningen, Rotterdam, The Netherlands
Kunsthaus, Zürich, Switzerland
The Metzger Collection, Museum Folkwang, Essen, West Germany
The National Gallery, Berlin, West Germany
Emanuel Hoffmann Foundation, Basel, Switzerland
Museum am Ostwall, Dortmund, West Germany
Deutsche Bank, Frankfurt, West Germany
The National Museum of Contemporary Art, Seoul, South Korea
Fundacion Caja de Pensiones, Madrid, Spain

This catalogue

accompanies an exhibition of paintings by

Jiri Georg Dokoupil

from September 19 to October 21, 1989

at the Robert Miller Gallery

41 East 57th Street, New York

John Cheim, Director

in cooperation with

Ileana Sonnabend and Leo Castelli

All works are soot on canvas.

Designed by John Cheim.